DYSLEXIA BRAIN GAMES

Visual Recognition (1)
Symmetrical Patterns & Geometrical Shapes

Dyslexia Brain Games

From Failure to Success
The #1 choice workbooks for dyslexic students and for kids who learn differently.
Copyright © 2017 by Downhill Publishing LLC.
Designed by Ramón Abajo

Downhill Publishing LLC
80 Eighth Ave,. Ste. Mezzanine
New York, NY (USA)
info@Downhillpublishing.com
www.fonts4teachers.com

Trademark Acknowledgments:
Apple, Apple Macintosh and TrueType are registered trademarks of Apple Computer Inc. Windows is a trademark of Microsoft Corporation. Adobe Type Manager is a trademark of Adobe Systems Incorporated. Fontographer and Fonts Lab are trademarks of FontsLab LTD.

This software and/or books was designed with Adobe Suite, Fontographer 5.2 and FontLab 5.

Acknowledgments:
- CREATED BY AN AWARD WINNING TEACHER OF THE YEAR., Ramón Abajo, who has received many awards, including "Teacher of the Year" in 1990 (Desert Sands Unified School District, CA).

- DEVELOPED BY PROFESSIONAL EDUCATORS, GRAPHIC DESIGNERS AND SOFTWARE PROGRAMMERS. The Dyslexia Brain Games series primary focus is developing educational software resources for kids and educators. Thanks to Baldesca Cortés Blanco, Special Educator and Project Director; Teresa Oñate Editor and Graphic Designer; Carol Caicedo, Graphic Designer and Ruben Aldecoa, programmer.

News Flash
DownHill Publishing has licensed its acclaimed Fonts4Teachers program to ICON Group International to develop e-books in Africa, Asia, and Latin America. The project was created by Professor Philip M. Parker, INSEAD Chair Professor of Management Science, who is the inventor of the "smart-writing machine", an amazing device that has allowed ICON Group to publish more than 200,000. His "K to 12 +2" project aims to create educational texts (e-book and print) in all the world's languages, especially for the smaller languages ignored by traditional publishers. Mr. Parker is presently involved in a number of multilingual rural education projects around the world funded, in part, by the "Bill and Melinda Gates Foundation."

Downhill Publishing - Our Company
The executive software designer, Ramón Abajo has worked as a classroom teacher for almost 20 years. Ramón is the founder, a teacher and special educator who has worked at the elementary and secondary levels. He has received many awards, including "Teacher of the Year" in 1990 (Desert Sands Unified School District, California). As a result of his nearly 20 year teaching career Ramón experienced a need for uniform, easy-to-use , which was both effective and affordable for teachers.

Section 1: Trace Lines
Visual and Spatial Patterns

Instructions:

1. Look carefully at the boxes on the left.

2. Memorize the pattern of the bold lines.

3. Draw the same pattern in the boxes on the right.

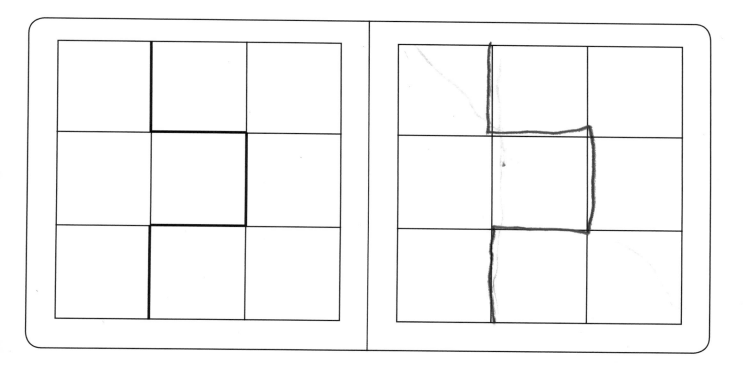

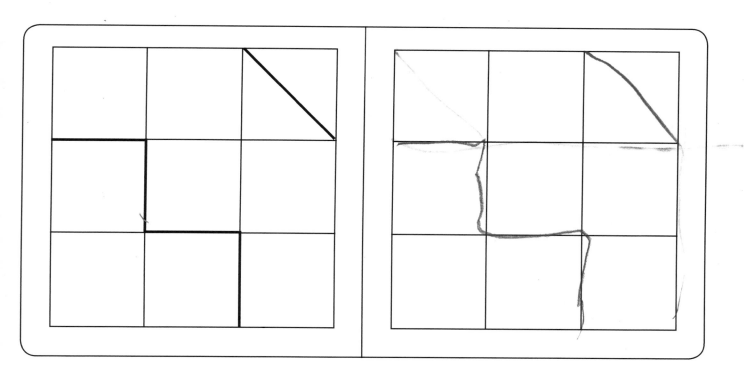

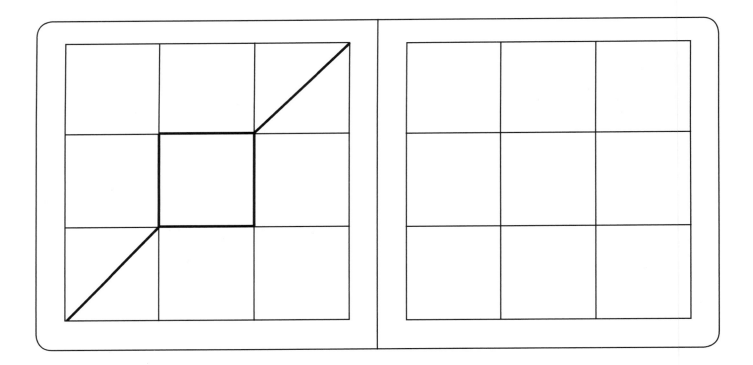

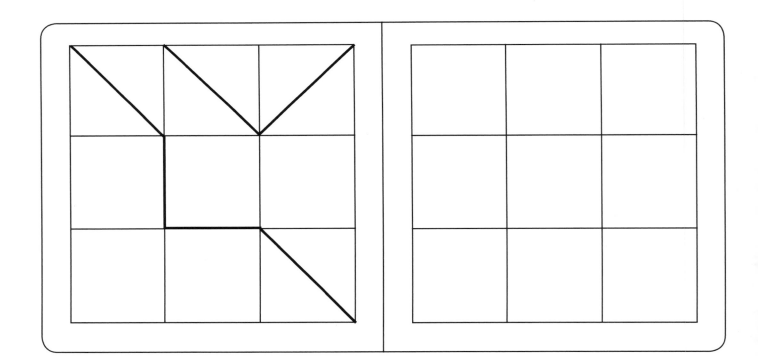

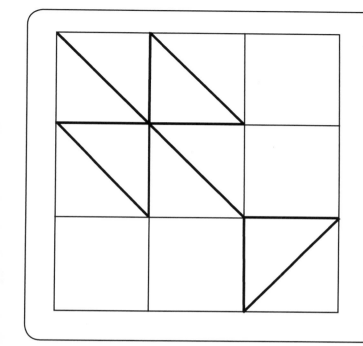 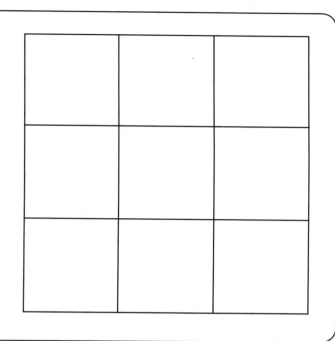

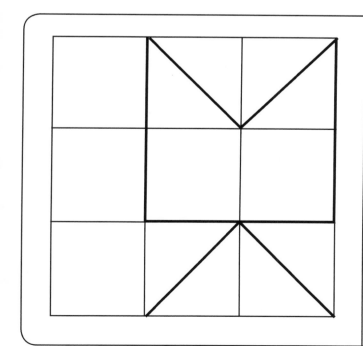 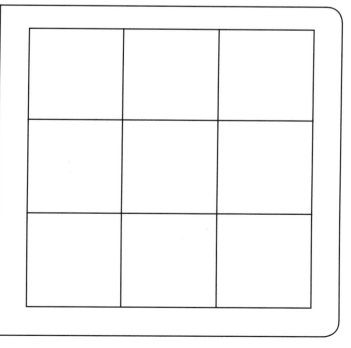

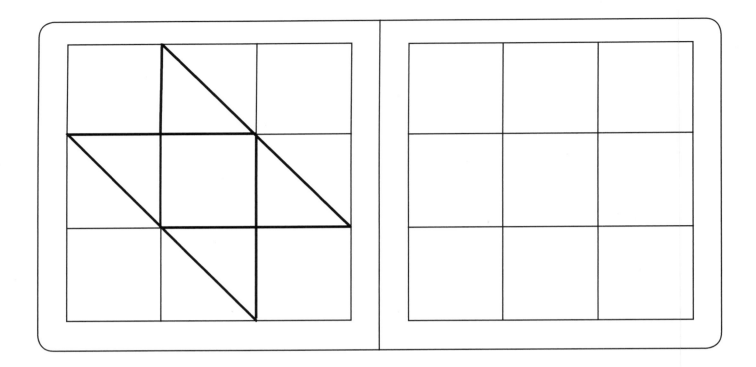

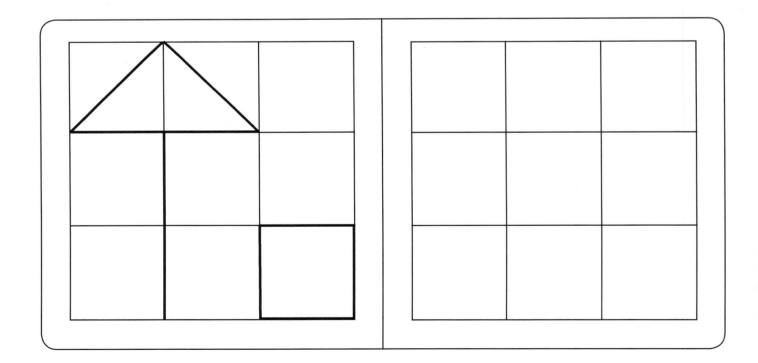

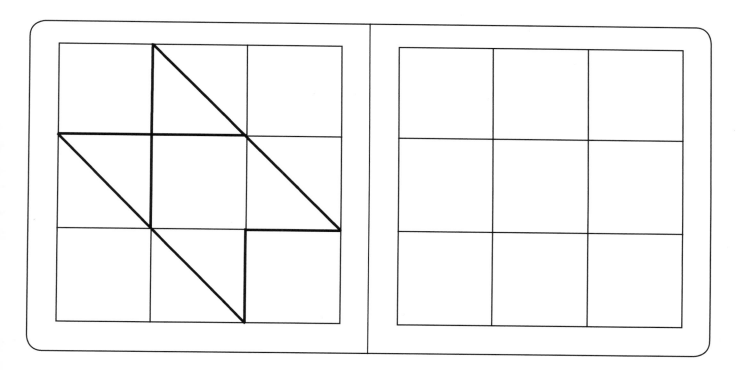

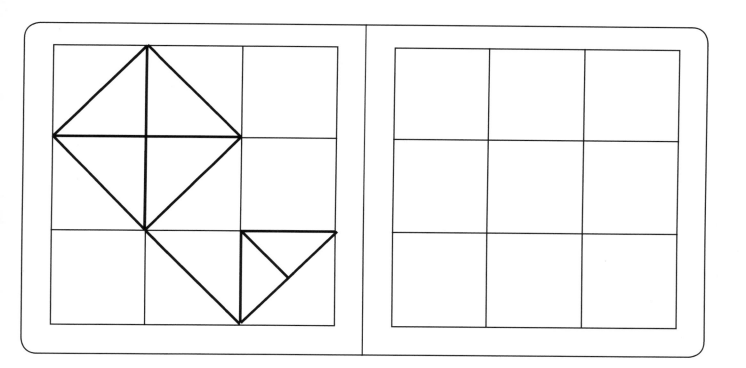

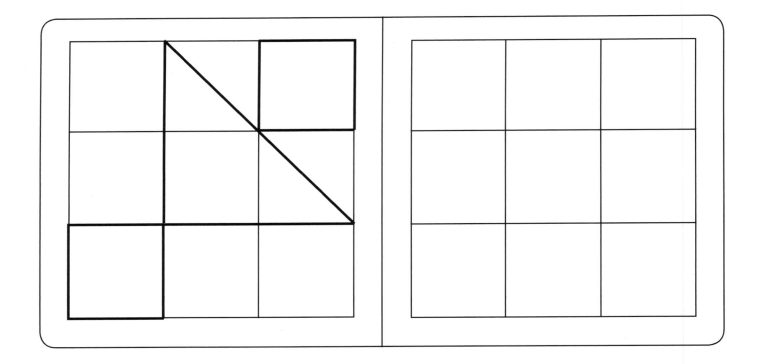

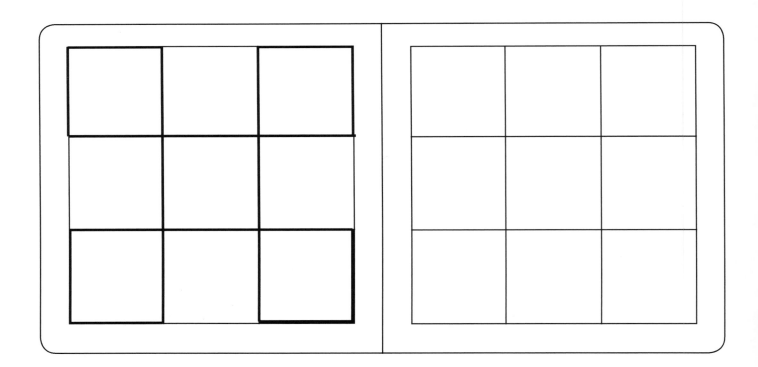

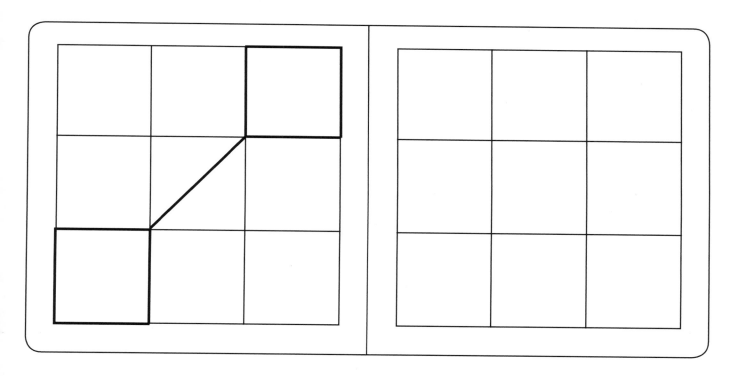

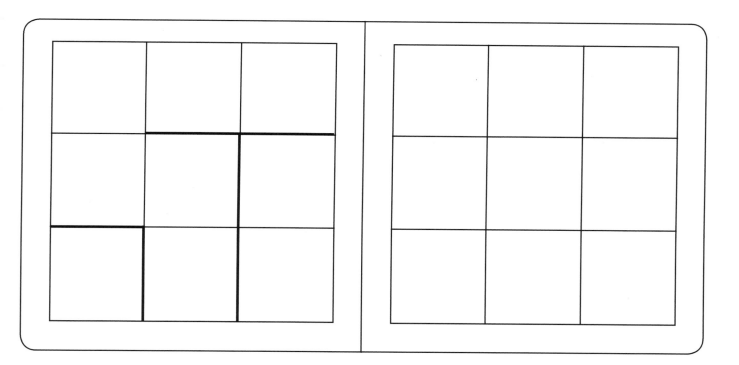

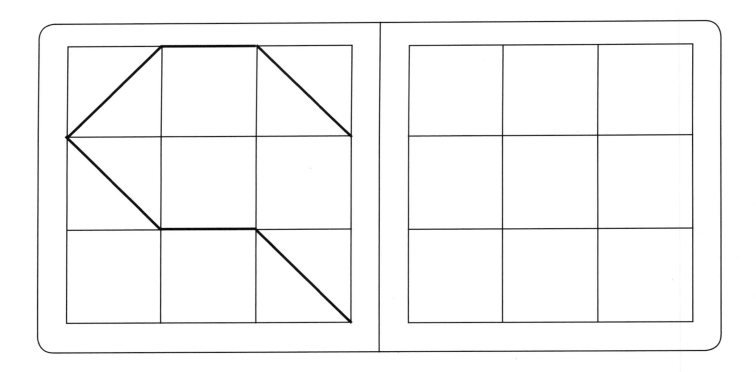

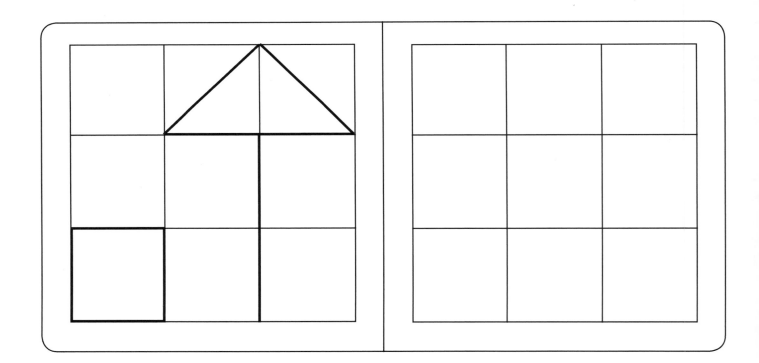

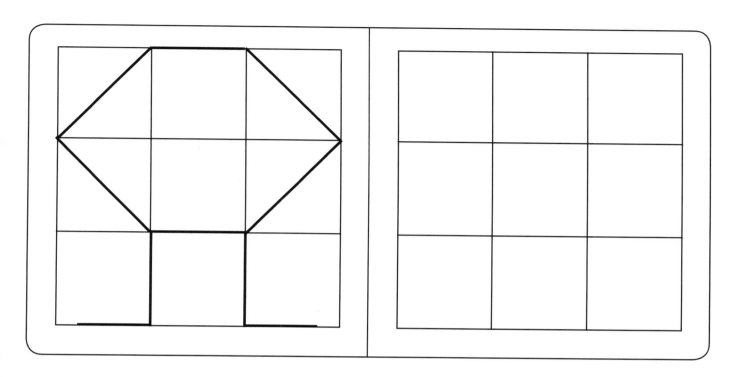

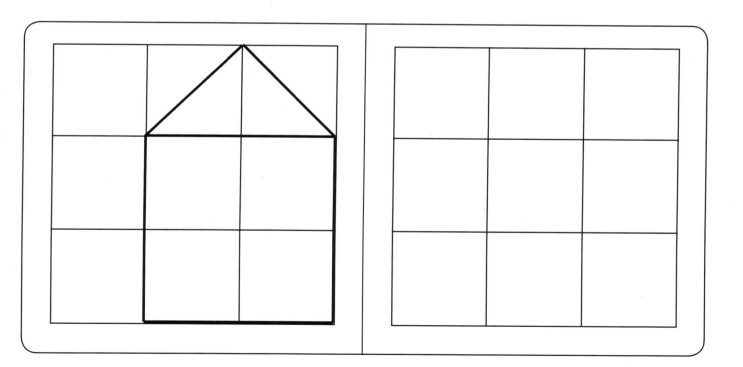

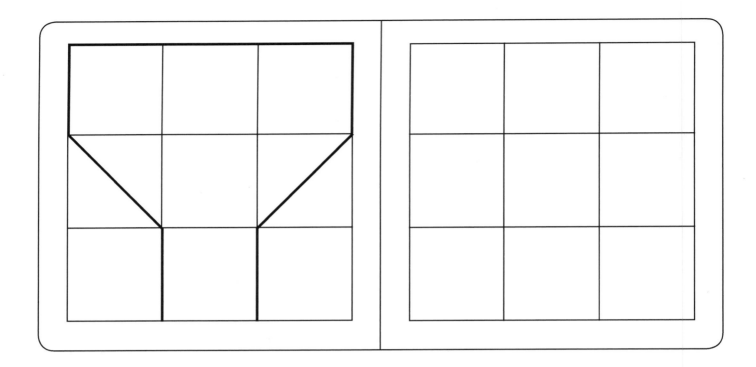

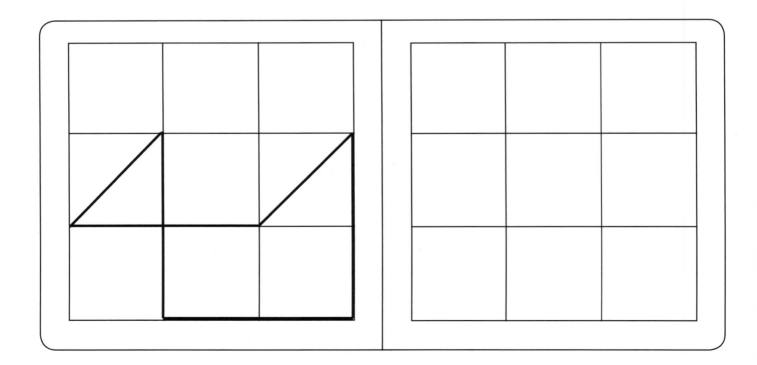

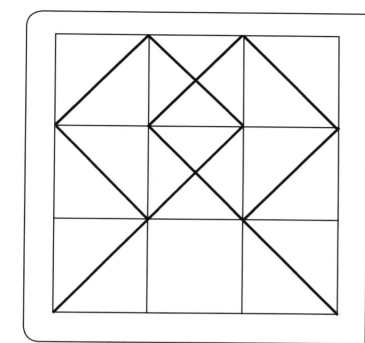
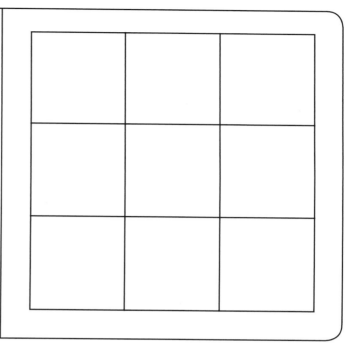

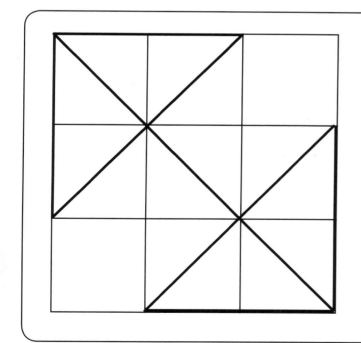
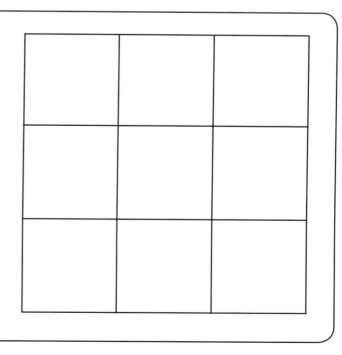

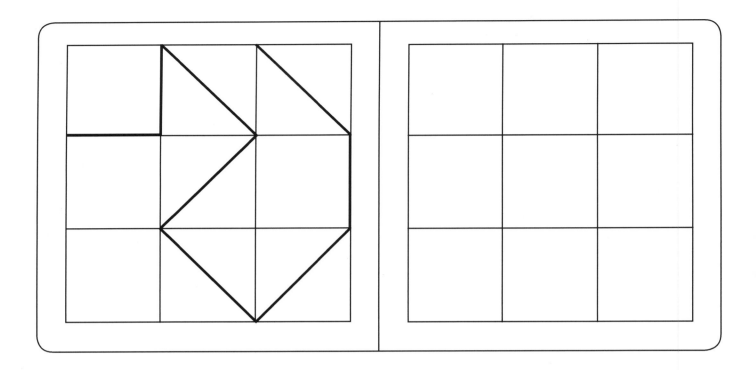

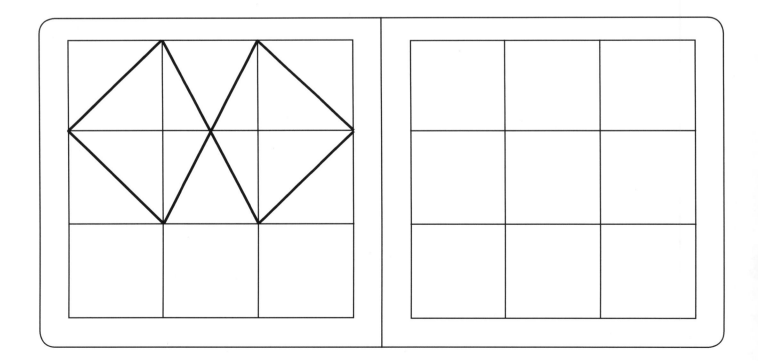

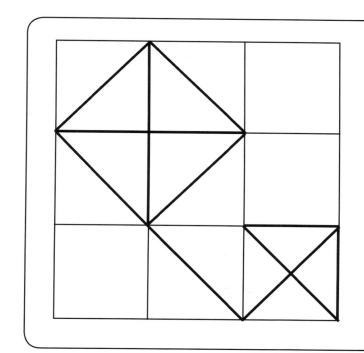
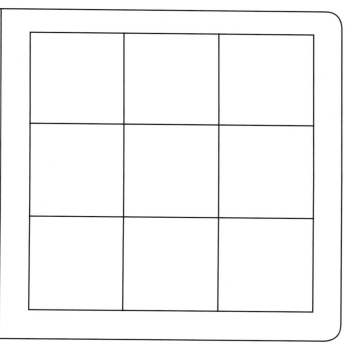

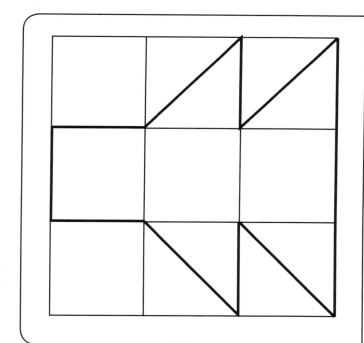
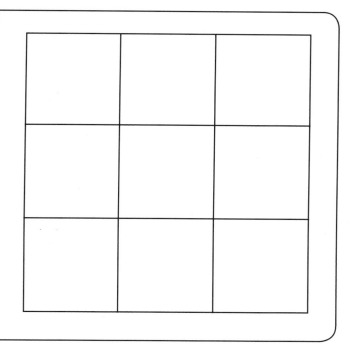

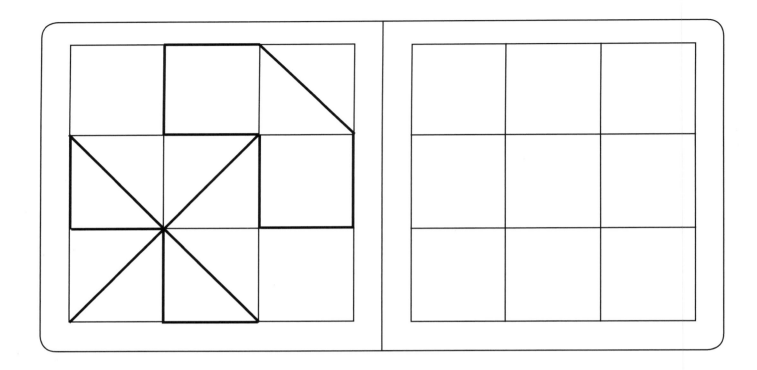

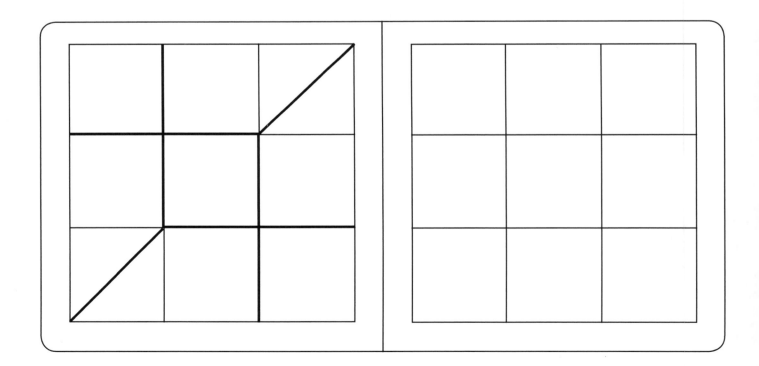

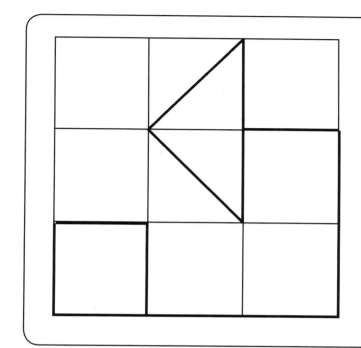
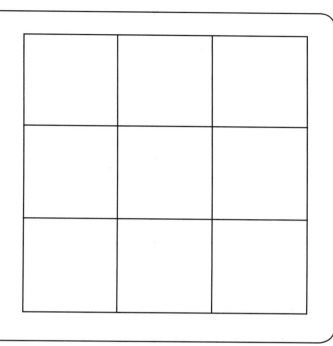

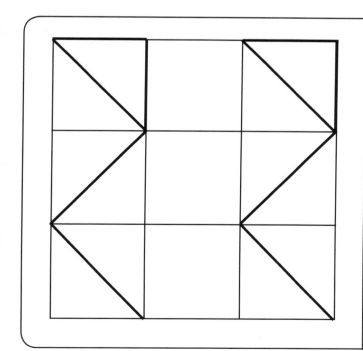
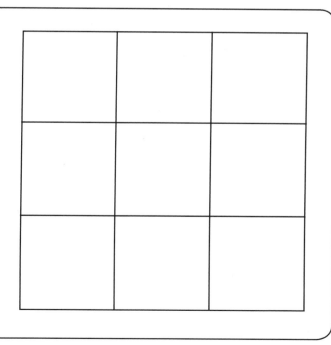

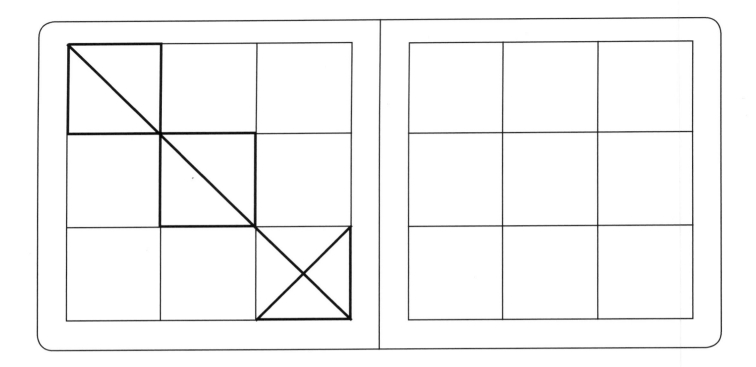

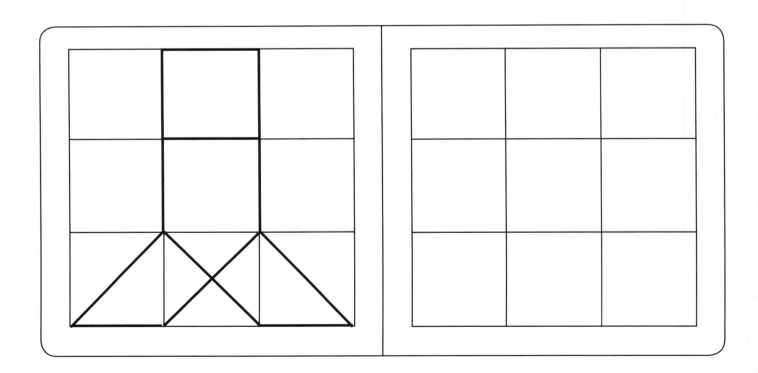

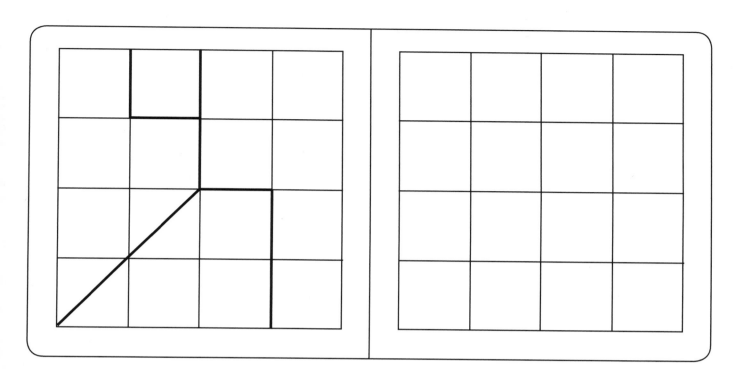

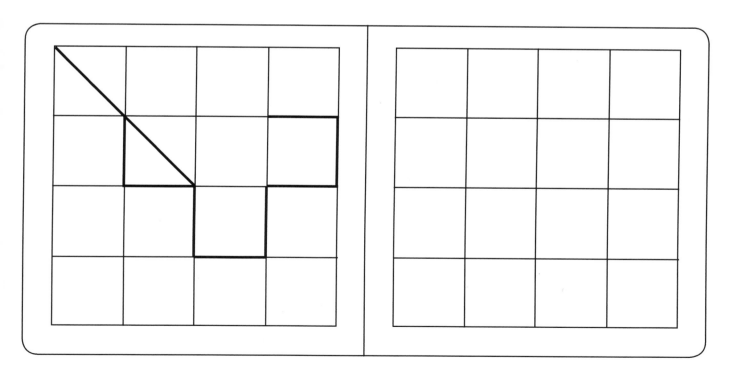

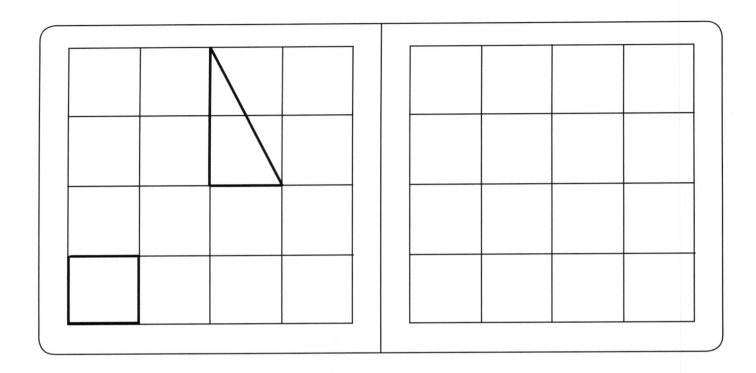

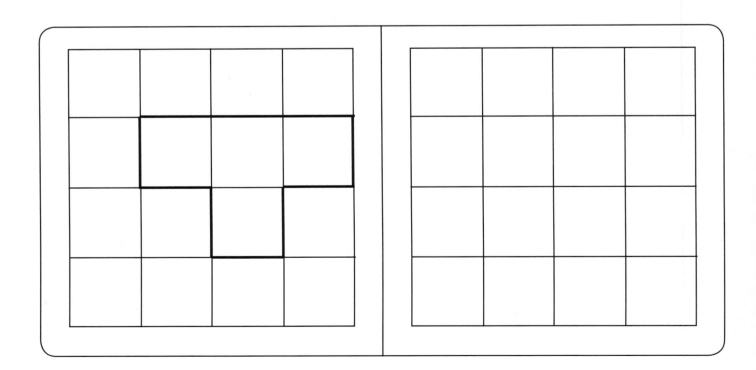

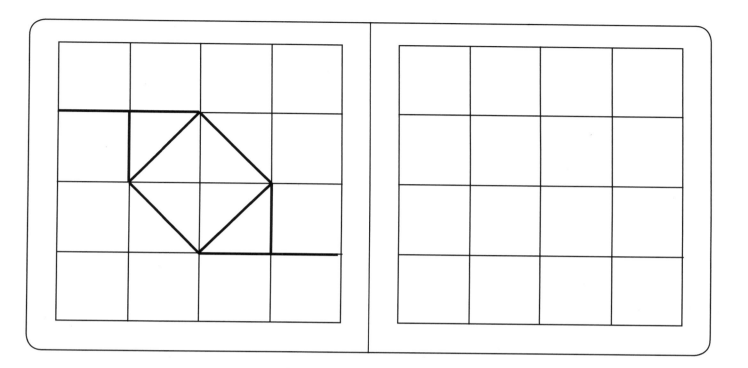

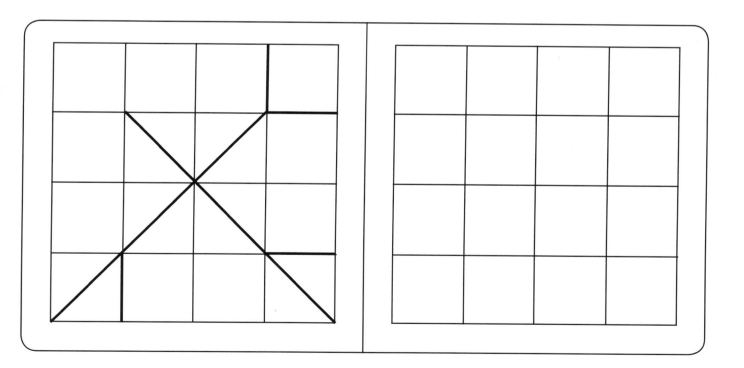

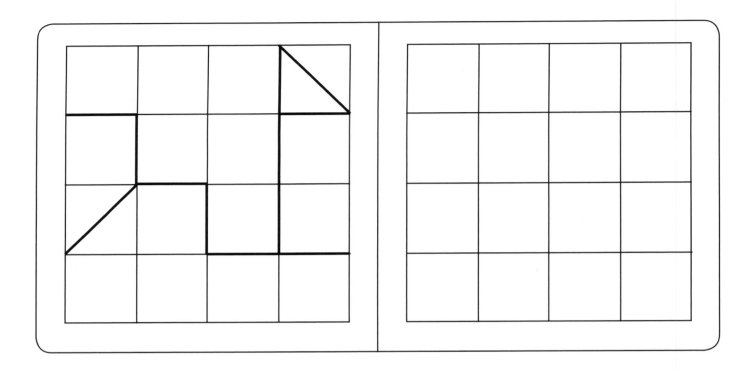

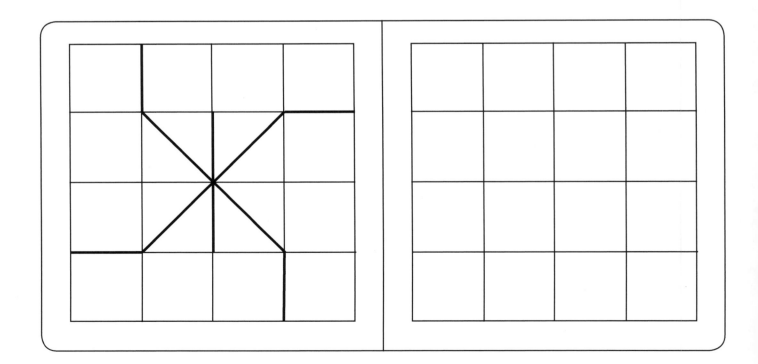

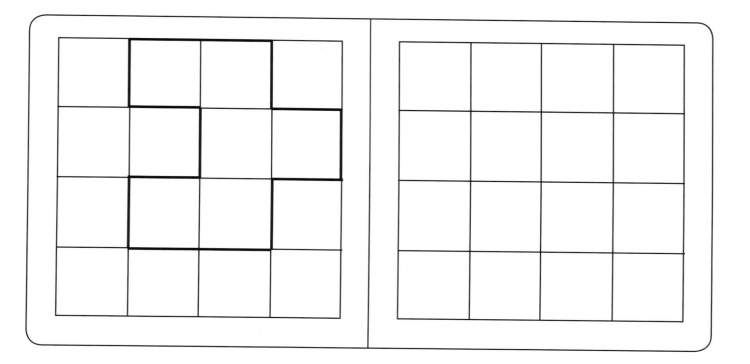

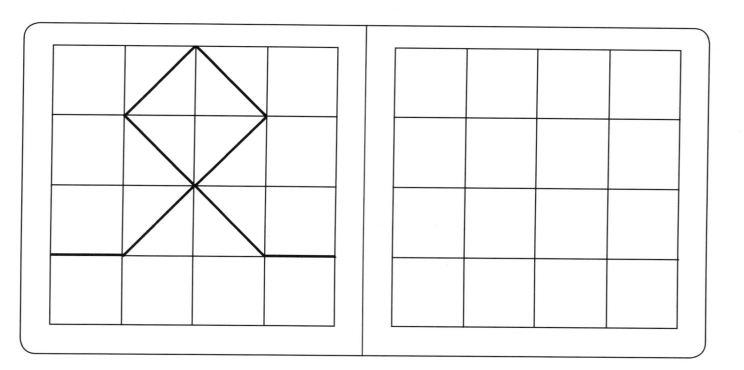

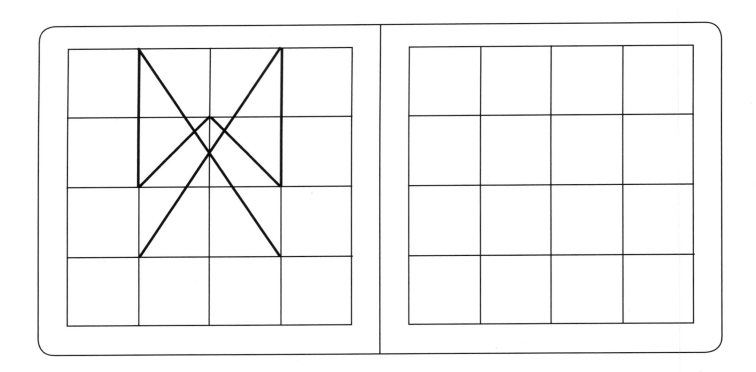

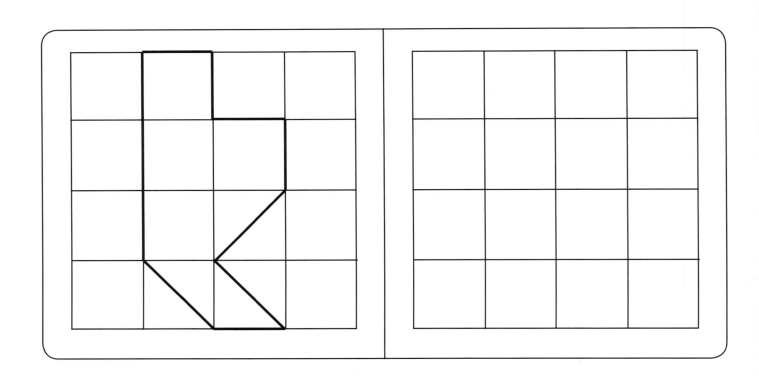

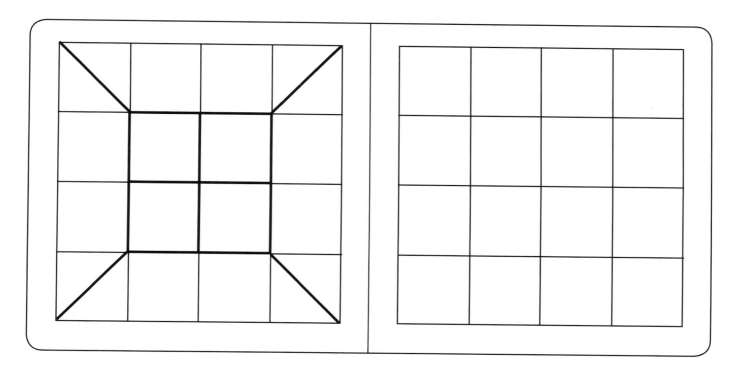

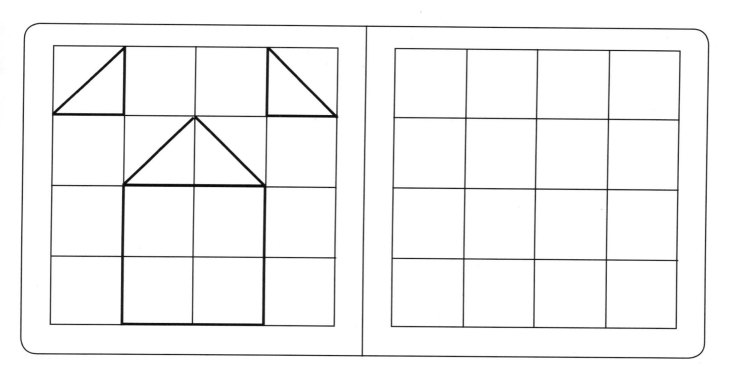

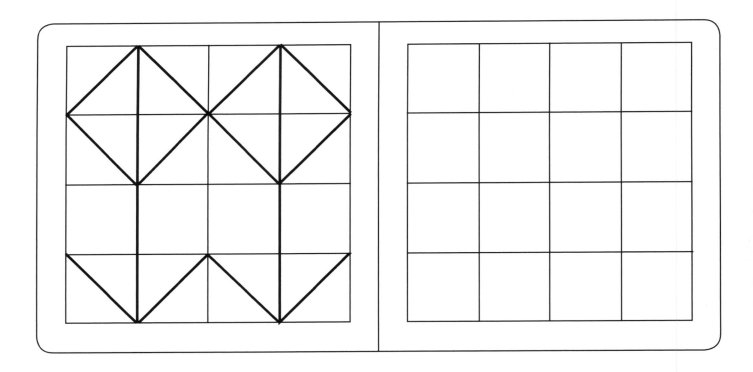

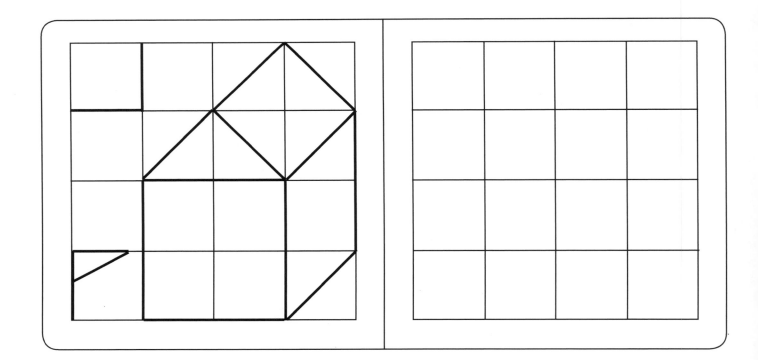

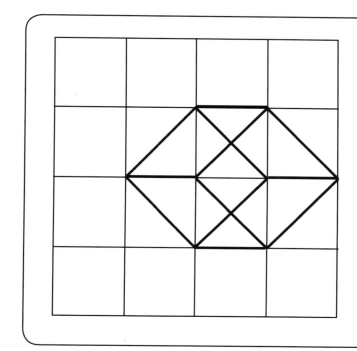 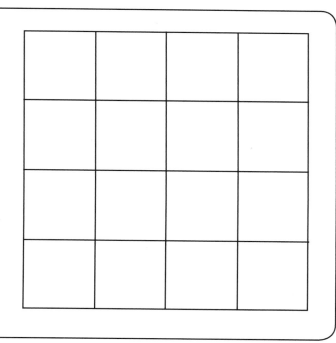

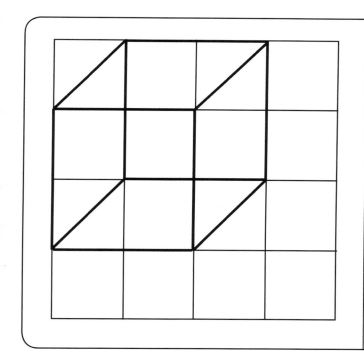 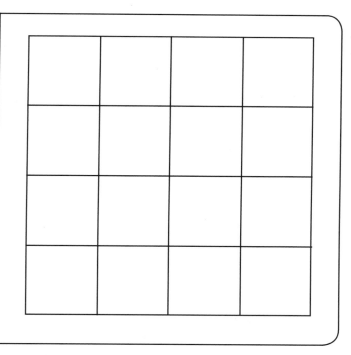

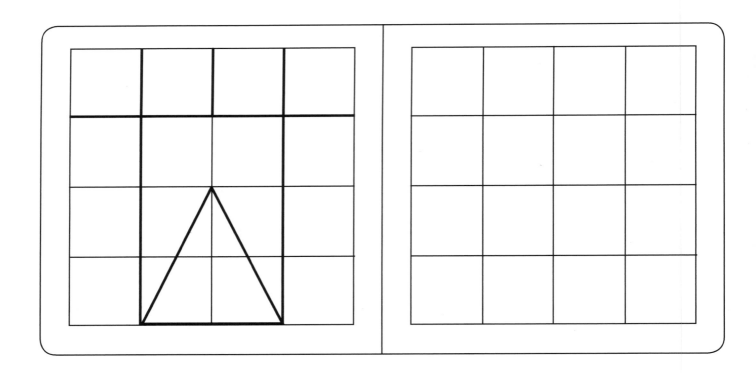

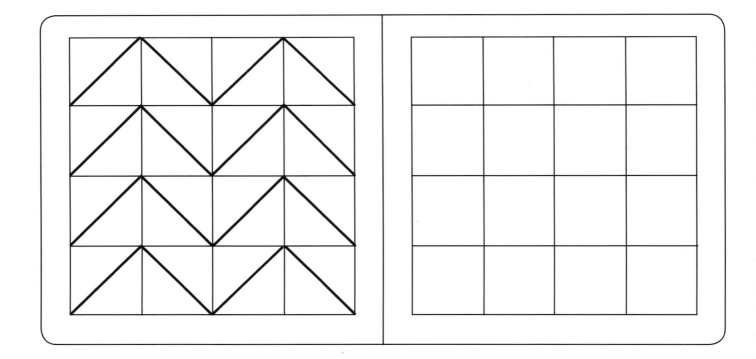

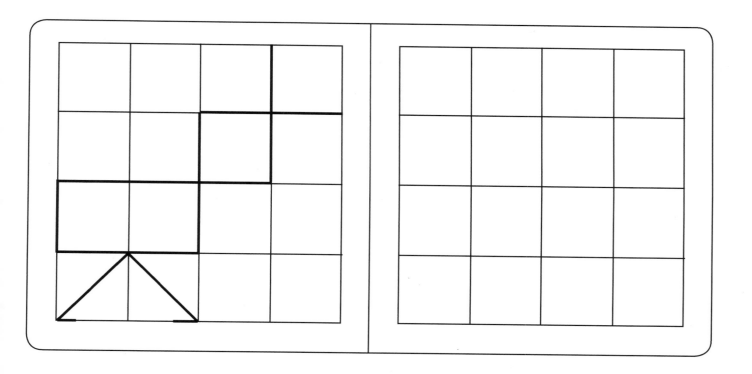

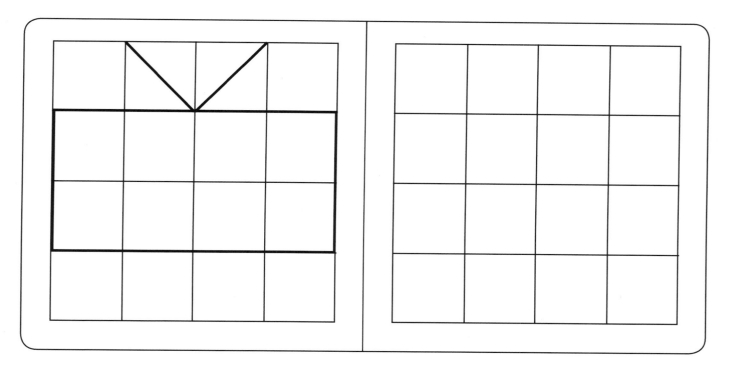

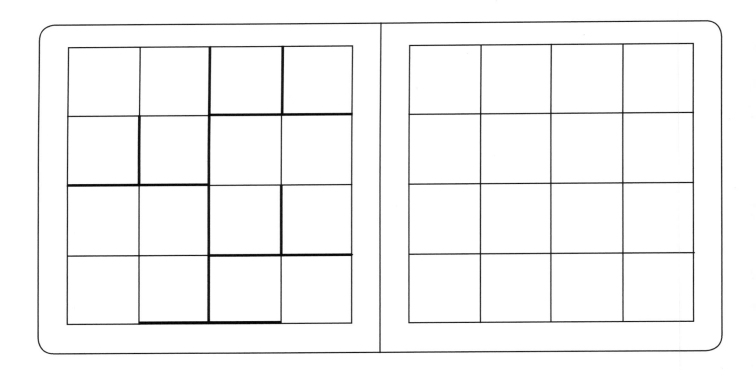

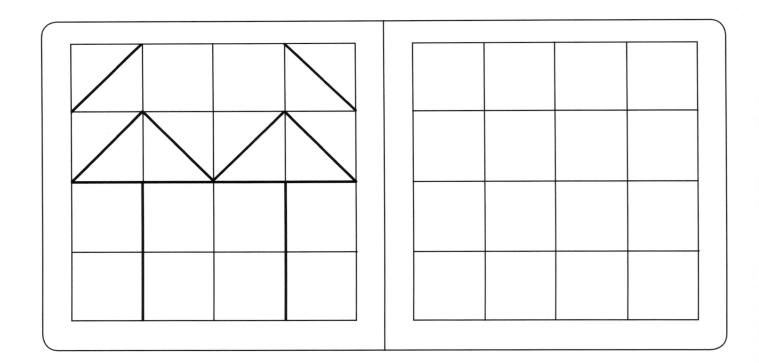

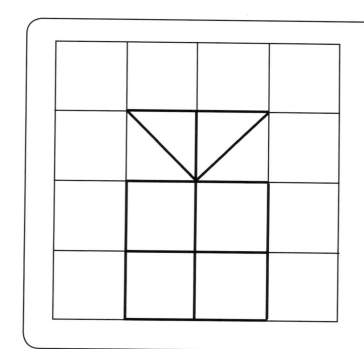
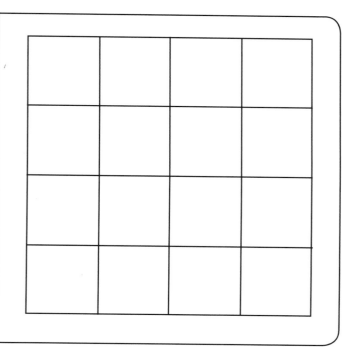

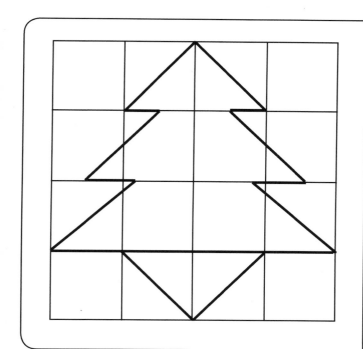
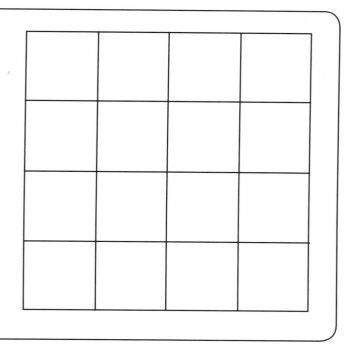

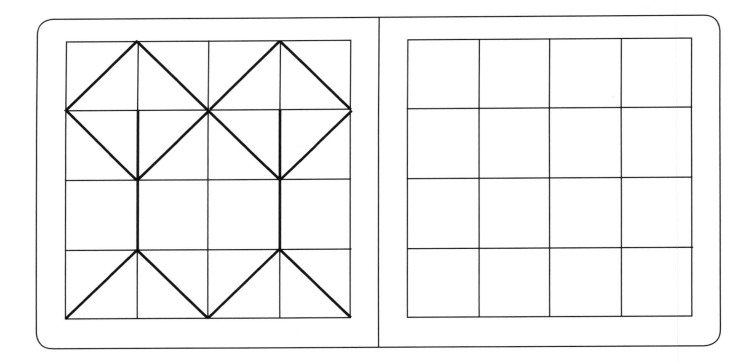

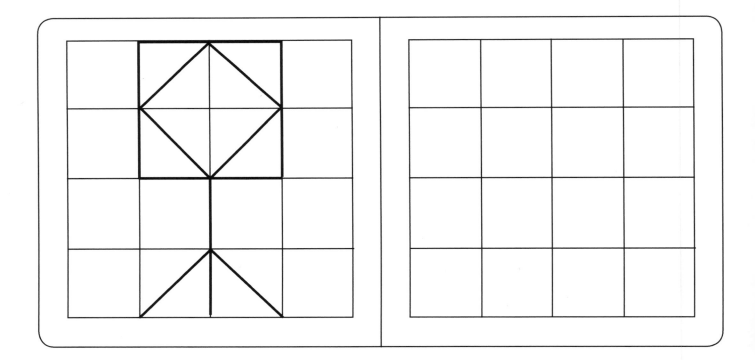

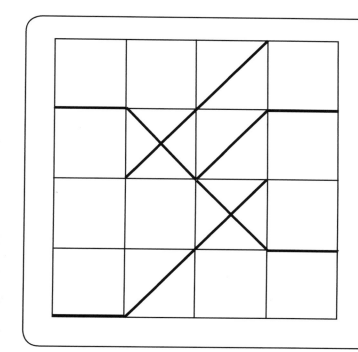
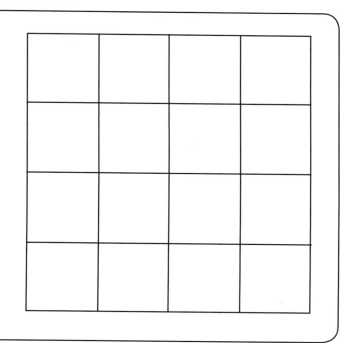

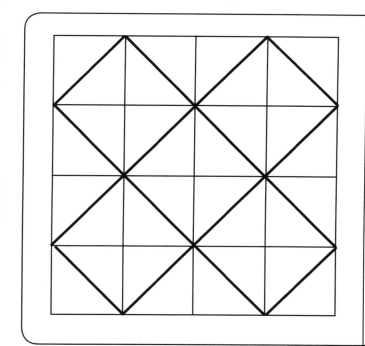
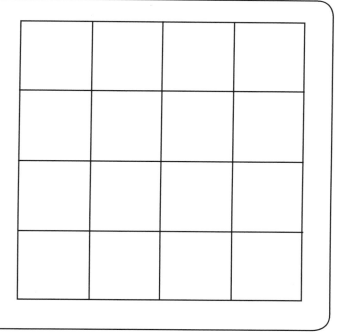

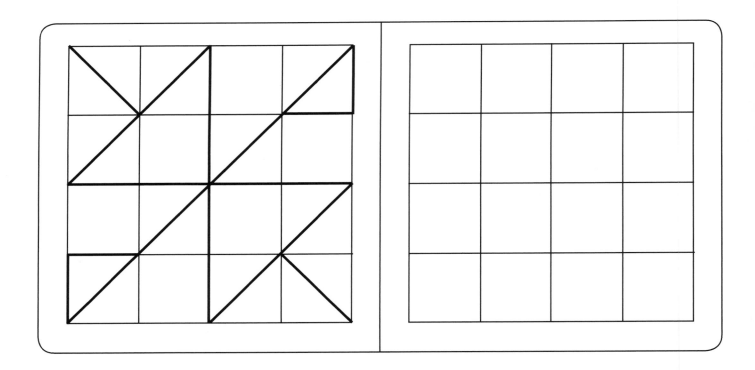

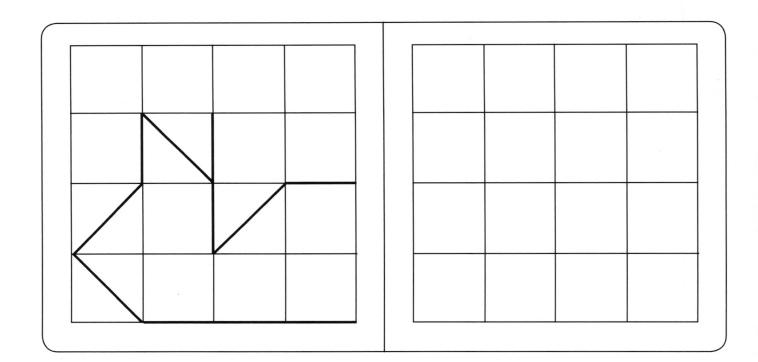

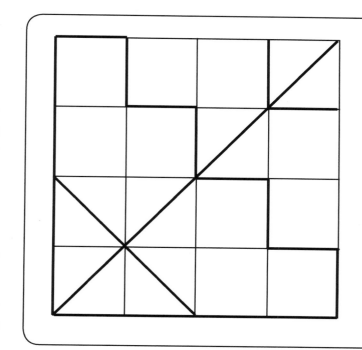
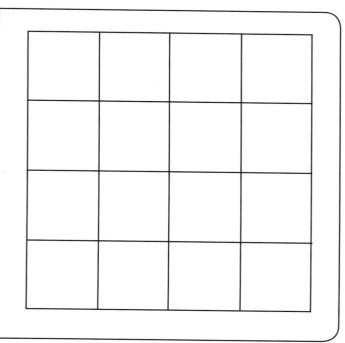

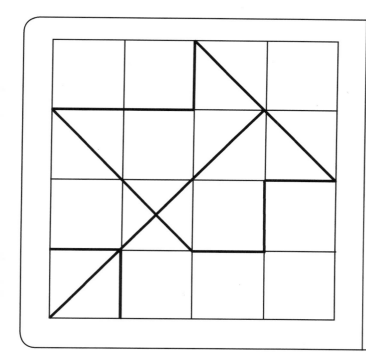
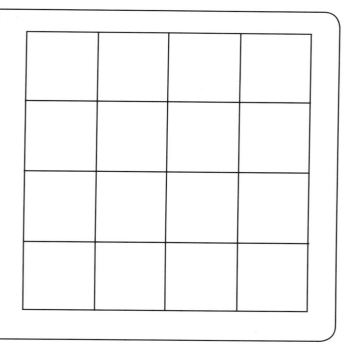

Name: ______________________________ Date: ______________

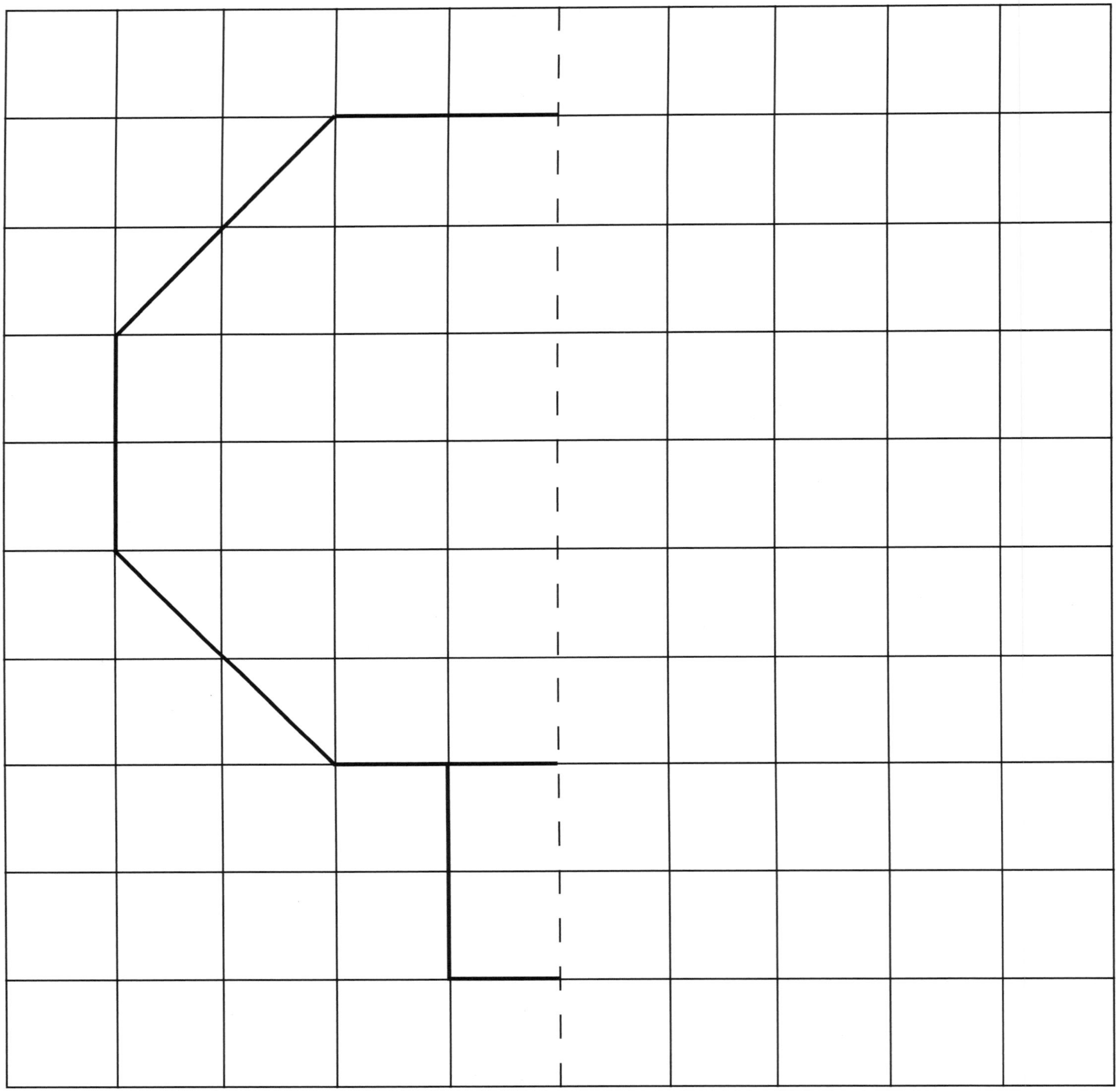

Name: ______________________ Date: ______________

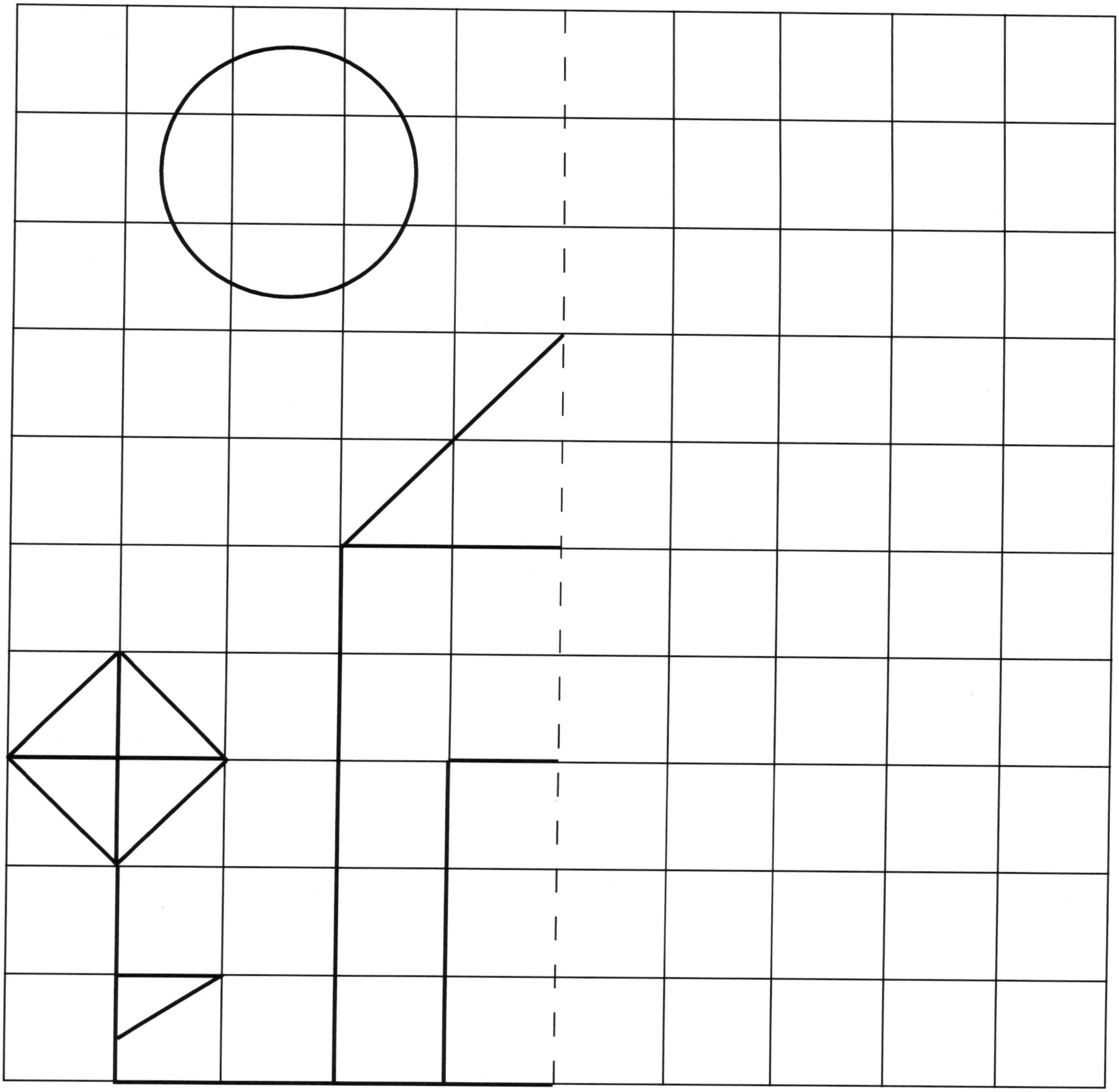

Name: ______________________ Date: ____________

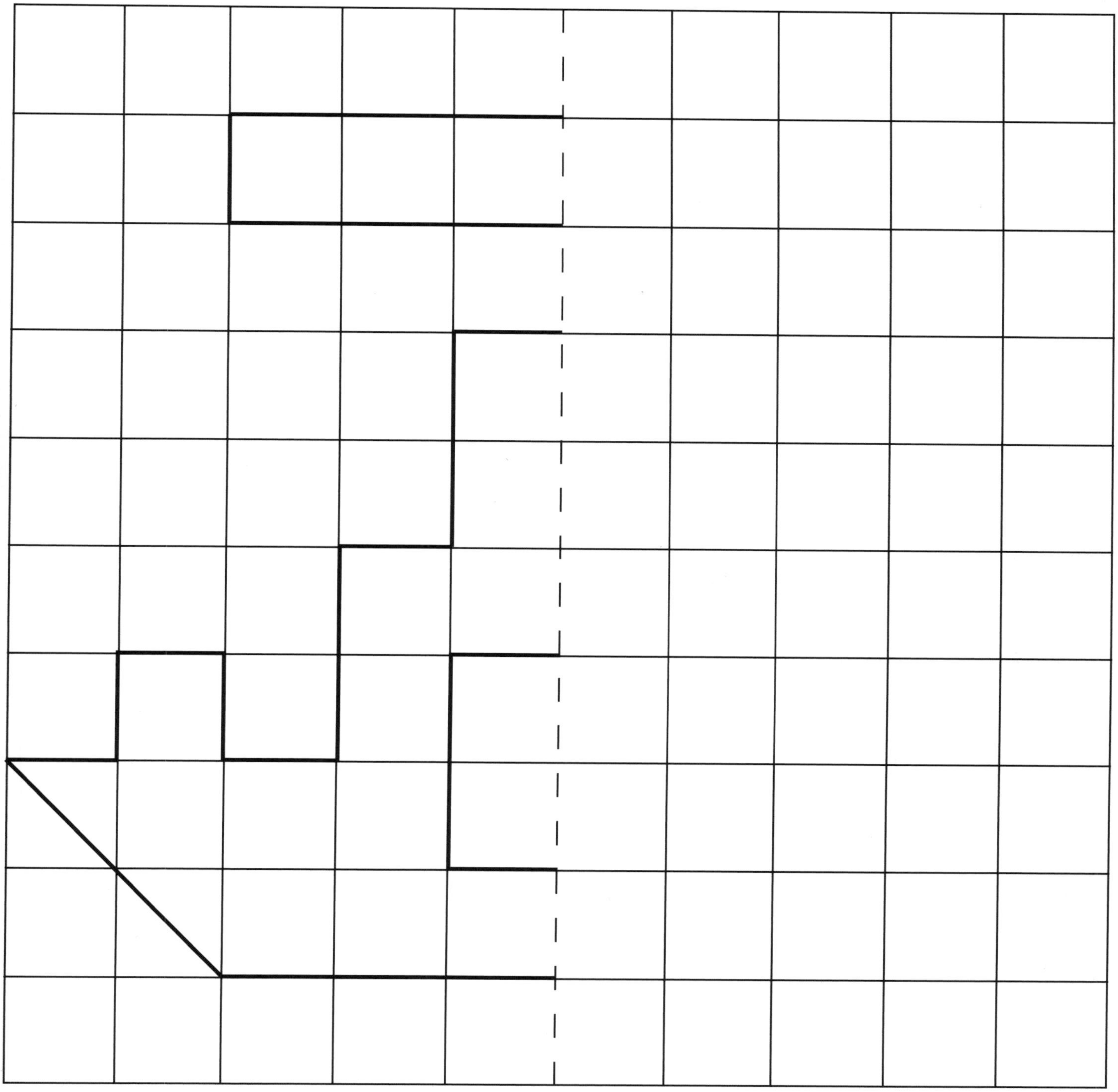

Name: ______________________________ Date: ______________

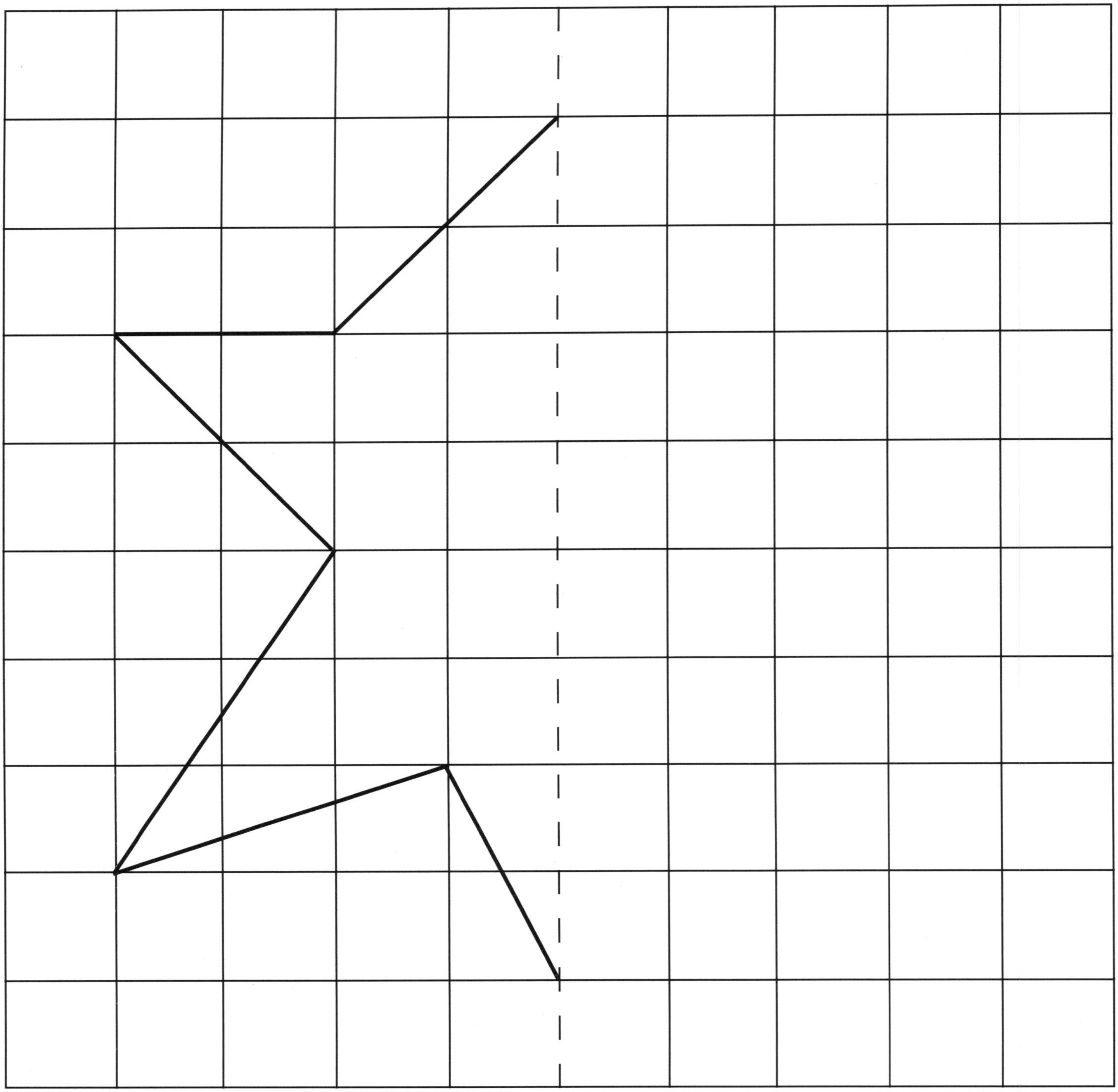

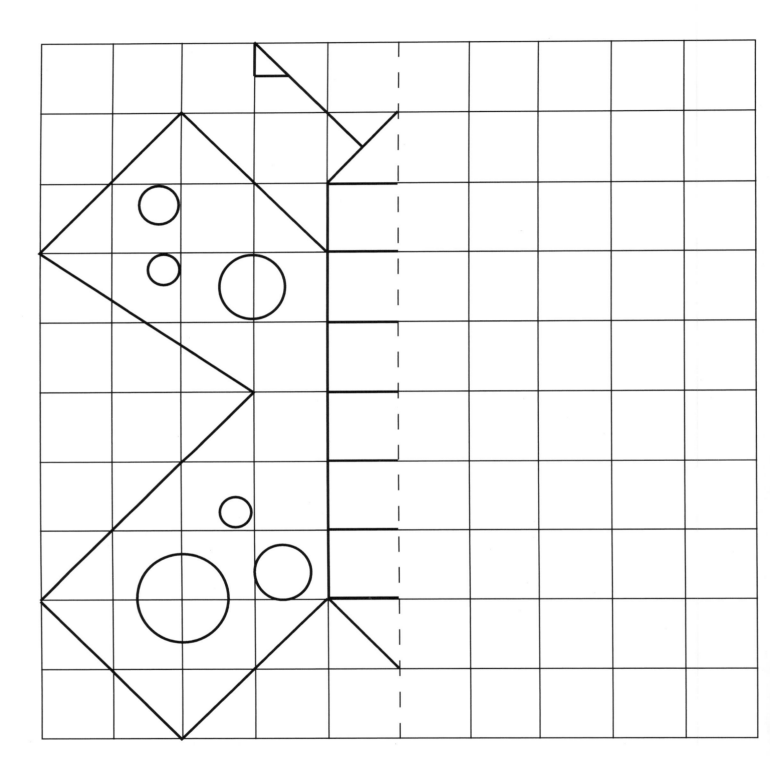

Name: ______________________________ Date: ______________

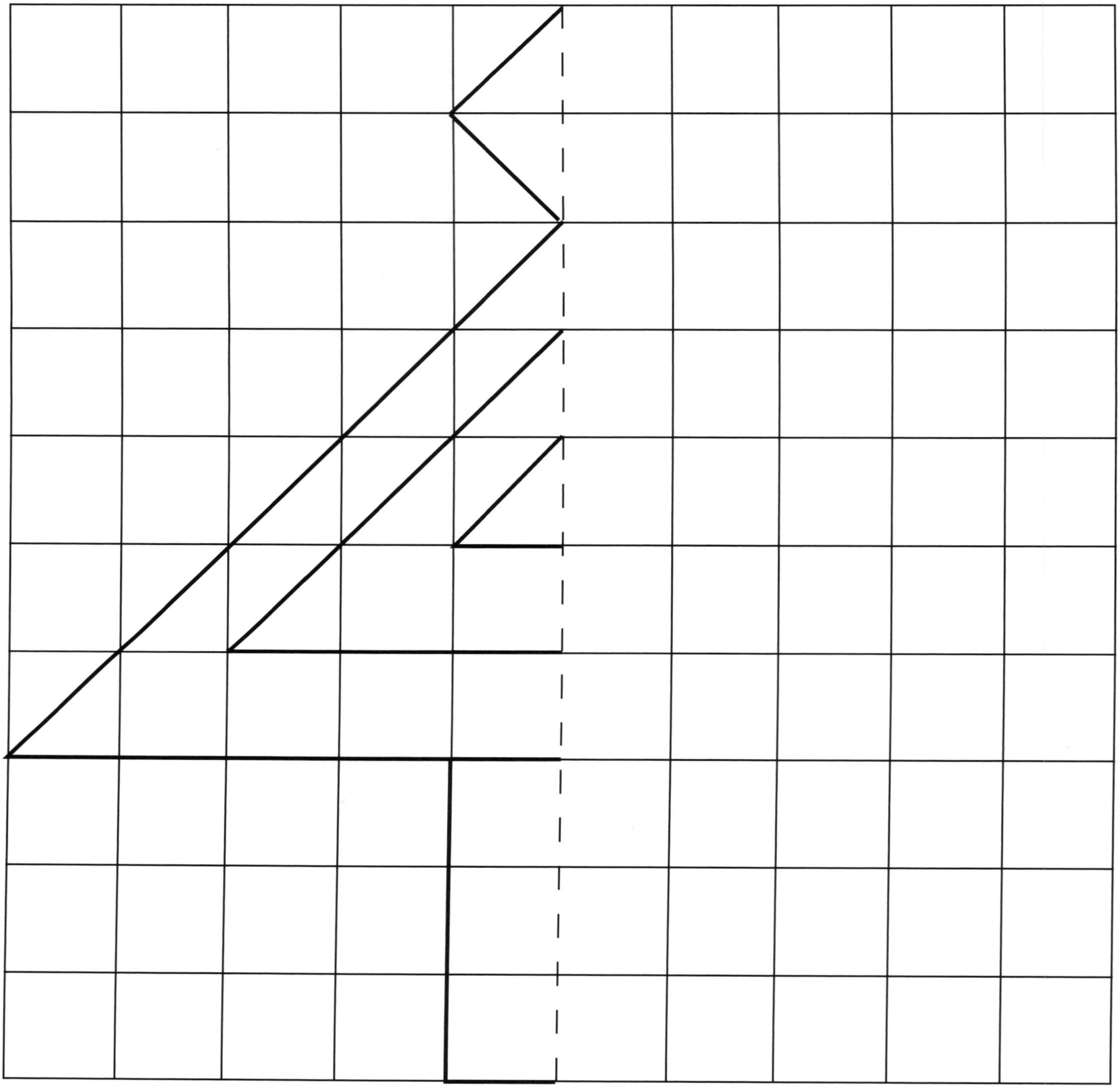

Section 2: Basic Shapes
Visual Recognition and Patterns

Basic shapes. Circle.

Basic shapes. Square.

Basic shapes. Triangle.

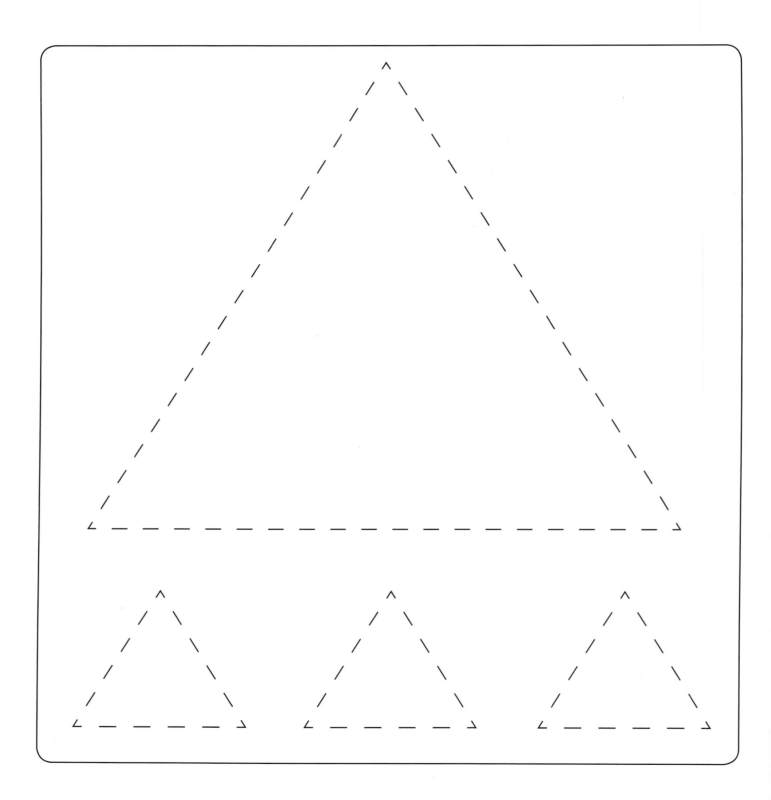

Basic shapes. Rectangle.

Basic shapes. Hexagon.

Color, trace, and connect the dots.

Color, trace, and connect the dots.

Name: _____   Date: _____

Color, trace, and connect the dots.

Color, trace, and connect the dots.

Color, trace, and connect the dots.

Count the squares. How many are there? _____.

Name: _____   Date: _____

Color the biggest square red.

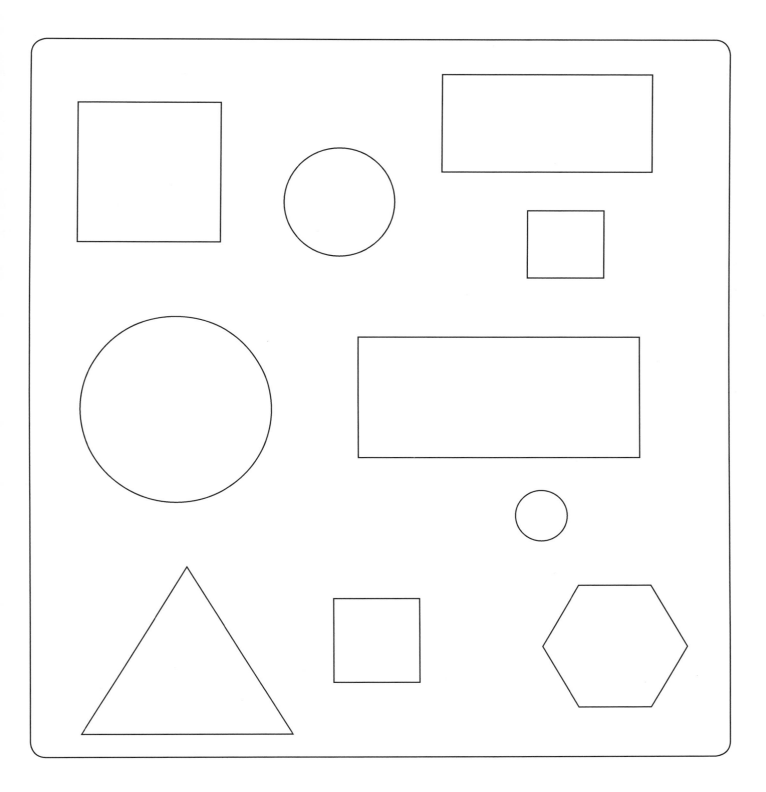

Name: _____   Date: _____

Count the circles. How many are there? _____.

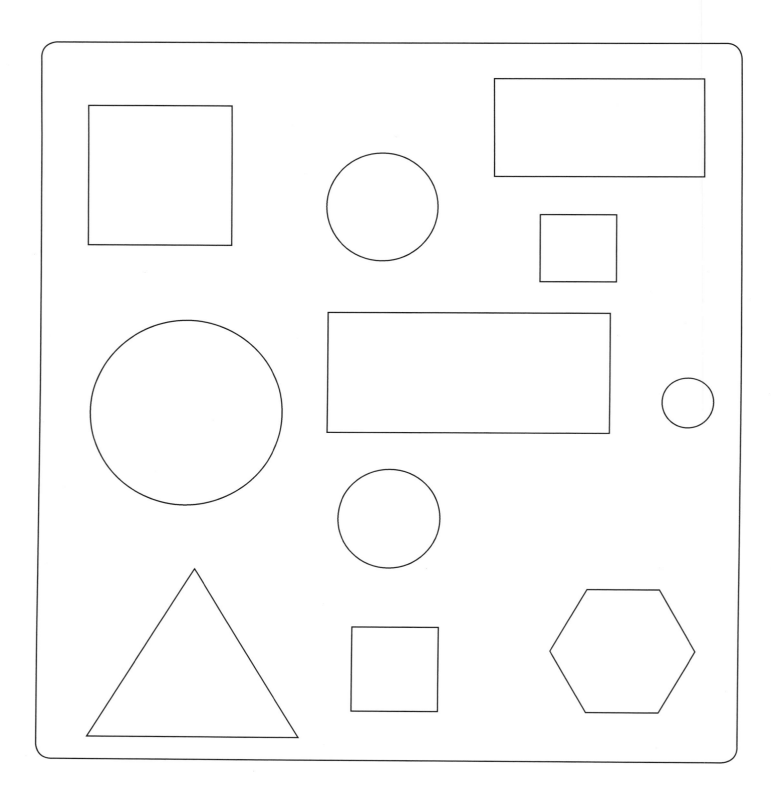

Name: _____ **Date:** _____

Color the biggest circle red.

Color the smallest circle blue.

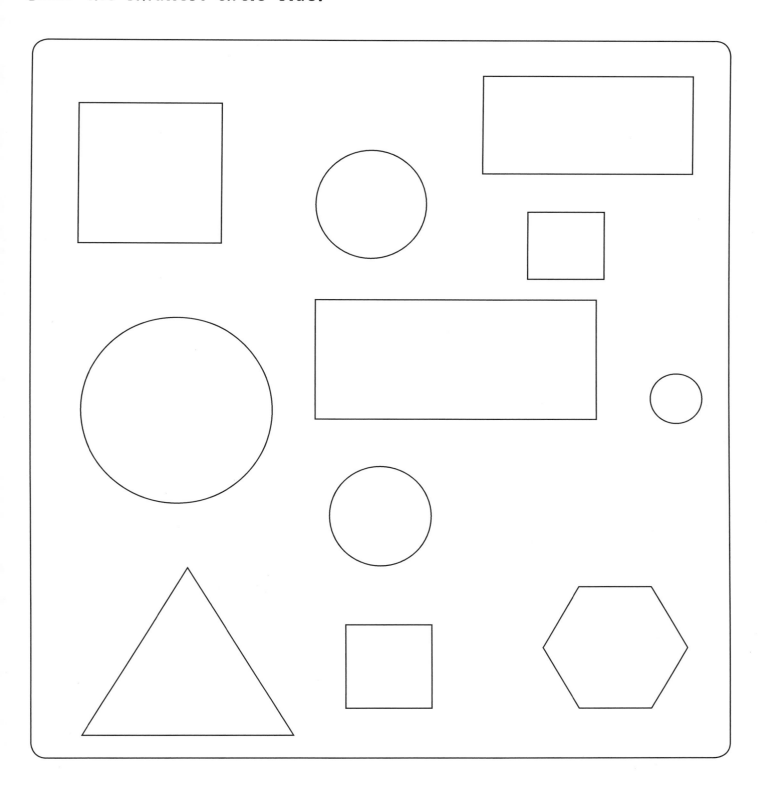

Name: _____   **Date:** _____

Count the rectangles. How many are there? _____.

Color them green.

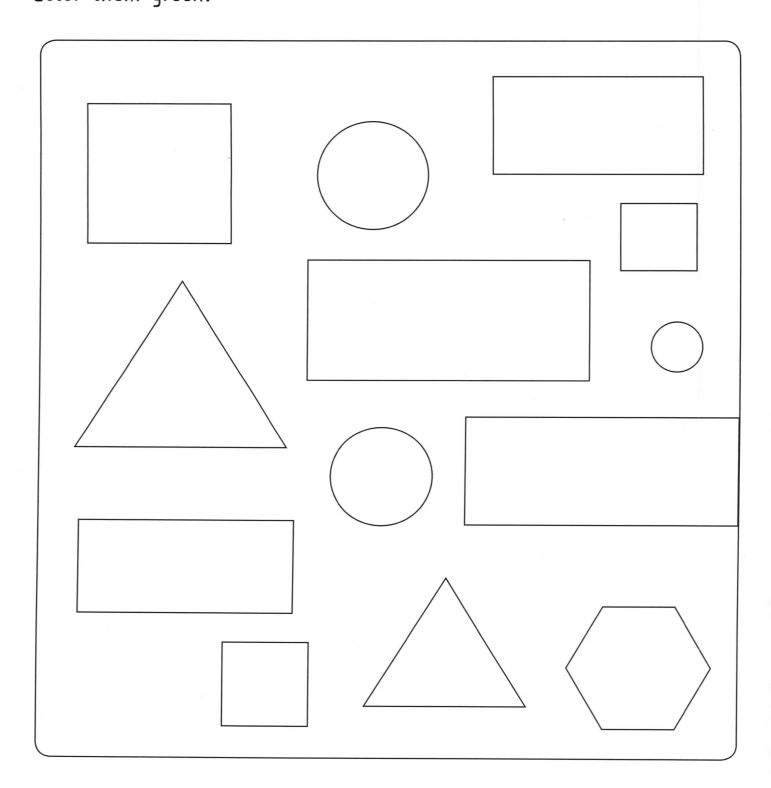

Name: _____ Date: _____

Color the squares blue.

Color the rectangles red.

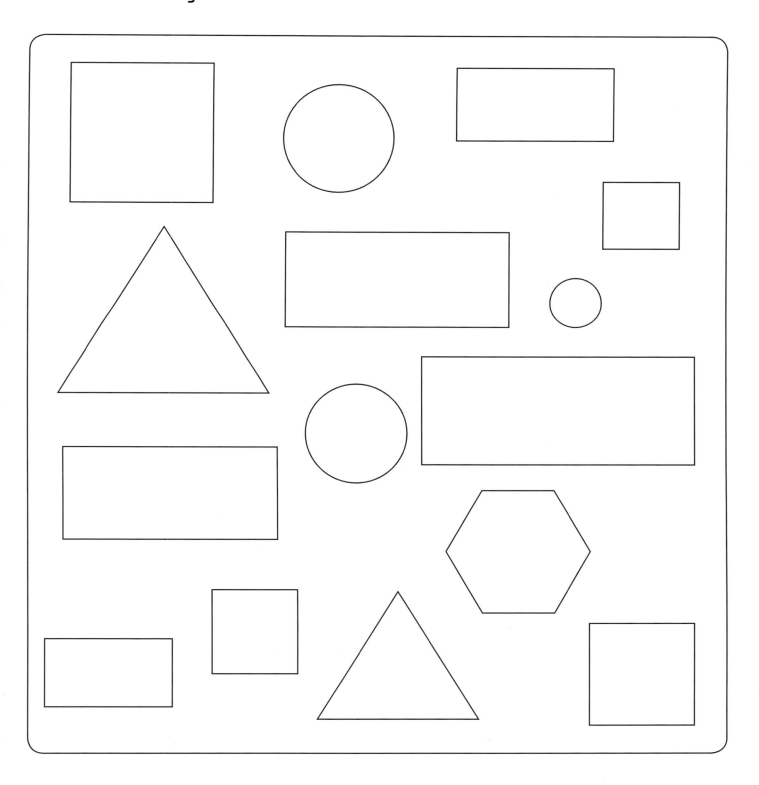

Name: _____   Date: _____

Count the triangles. How many are there? _____.

Color them yellow.

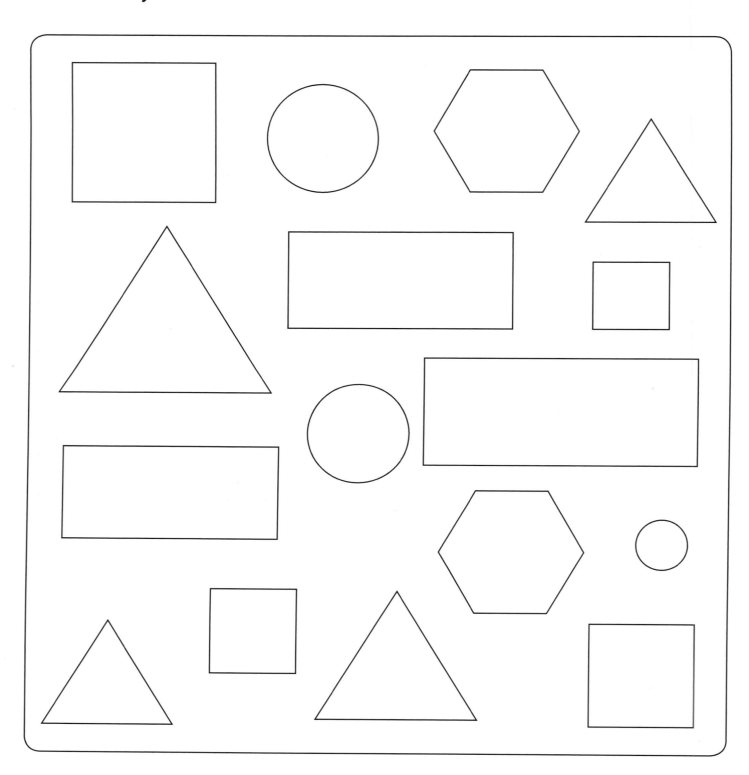

Name: _____   Date: _____

Color the biggest triangle green.

Color the smallest triangle red.

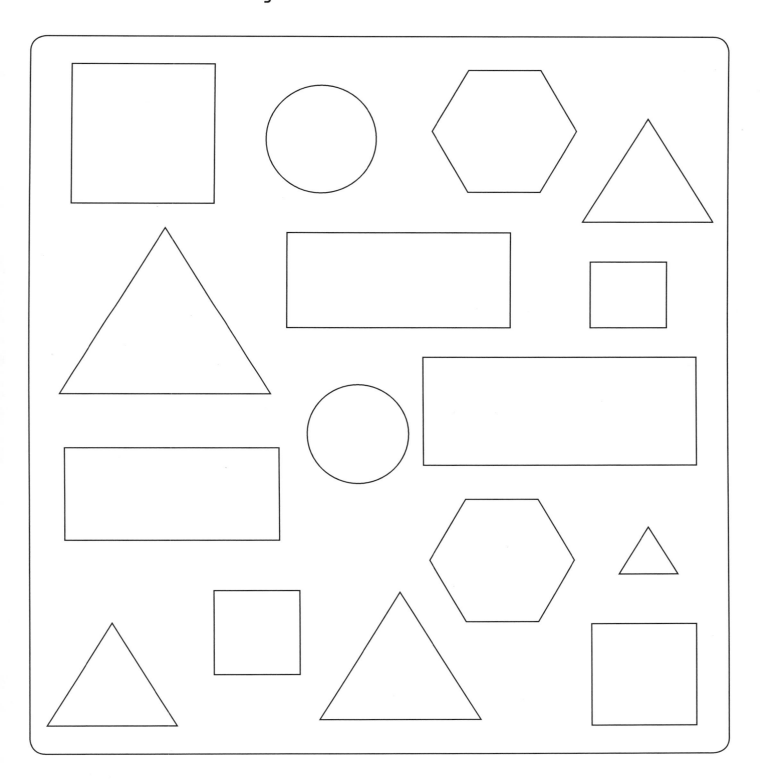

Name: _____ Date: _____

Count the hexagons. How many are there? _____.

Color them blue.

Name: _____   Date: _____

Color the circles red.

Color the triangles yellow.

Name: _____   Date: _____

Color:

- the squares blue.   - the triangles red.

- the rectangles green.   - the circles yellow.

Color:

- the squares blue.

                                           - the triangles red.

- the rectangles green.

                                           - the circles yellow.

Name: _____ **Date:** _____

Color:

- the squares blue.

- the rectangles green.

- the triangles red.

- the circles yellow.

Color:

- the squares blue.   - the triangles red.

- the rectangles green.   - the circles yellow.

Name: _____   Date: _____

Color:

- the squares blue.   - the triangles red.

- the rectangles green.   - the circles yellow.

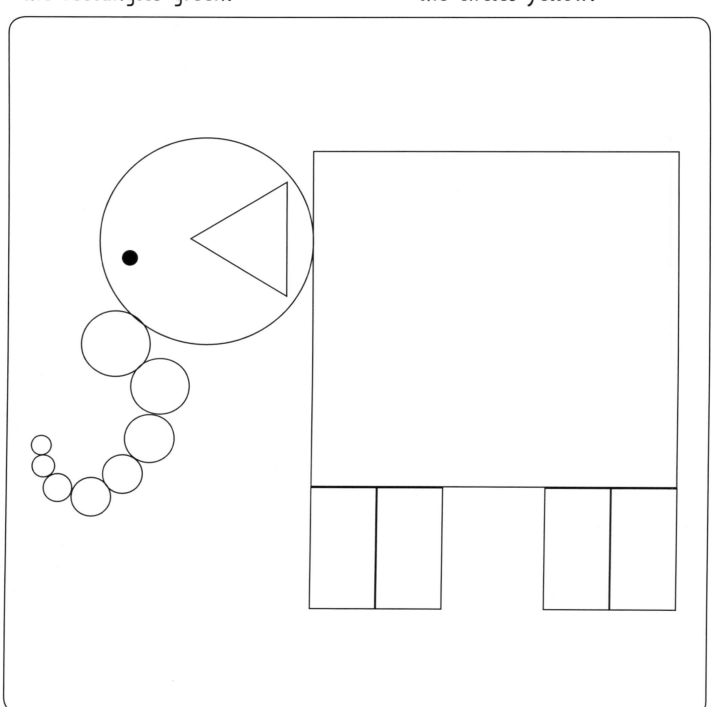

Color:

- the squares blue.   - the triangles orange.

- the rectangles green.   - the circles yellow.

Name: _____   Date: _____

Color:

- the squares blue.   - the triangles orange.

- the rectangles green.   - the circles yellow.

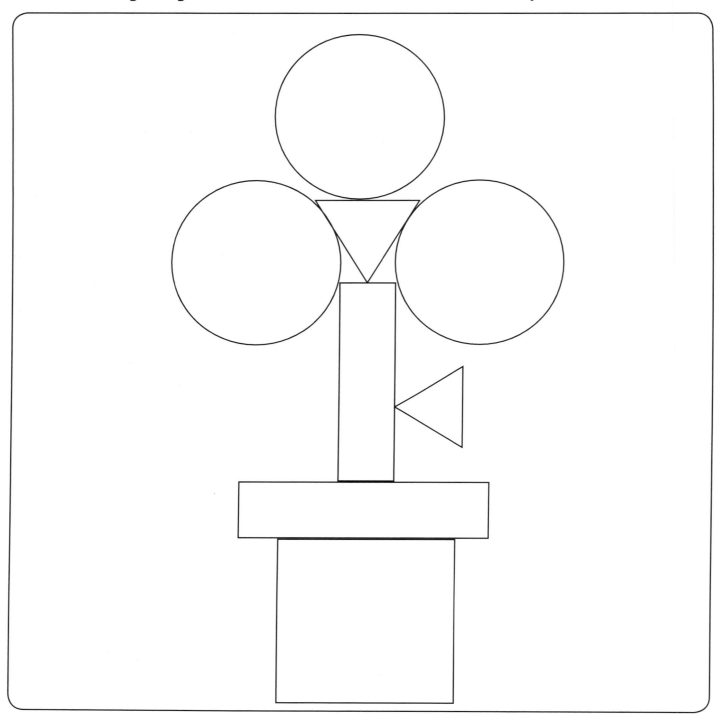

Name: _____   **Date:** _____

Color:

- the squares blue.

- the rectangles orange.

- the triangles yellow.

- the circles pink.

Name: _____   **Date:** _____

Color the boxes in the table following these rules:

- Squares are green.

- Triangles are yellow.

Name: _____ Date: _____

Color the boxes in the table following these rules:

- Rectangles are blue.

- Circles are red.

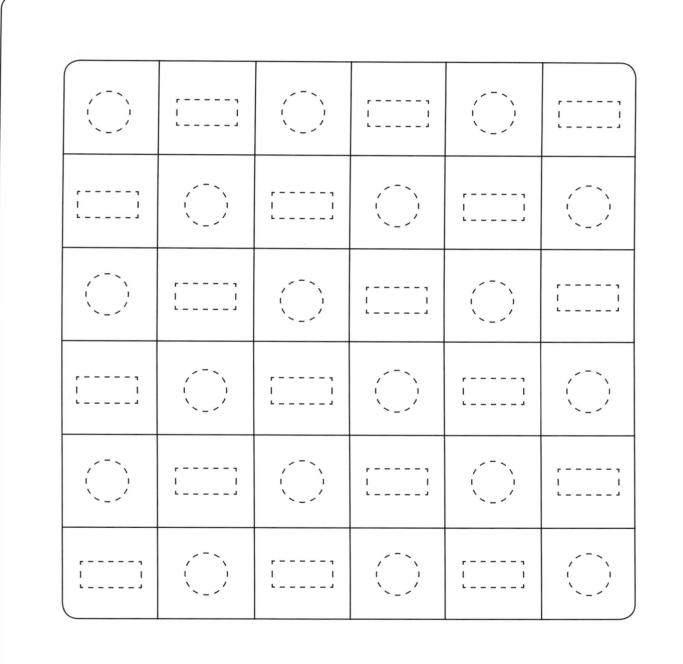

Name: _____   **Date:** _____

Color the boxes in the table following these rules:

- Triangles are blue.   - Hexagons are red.

- Circles are green.

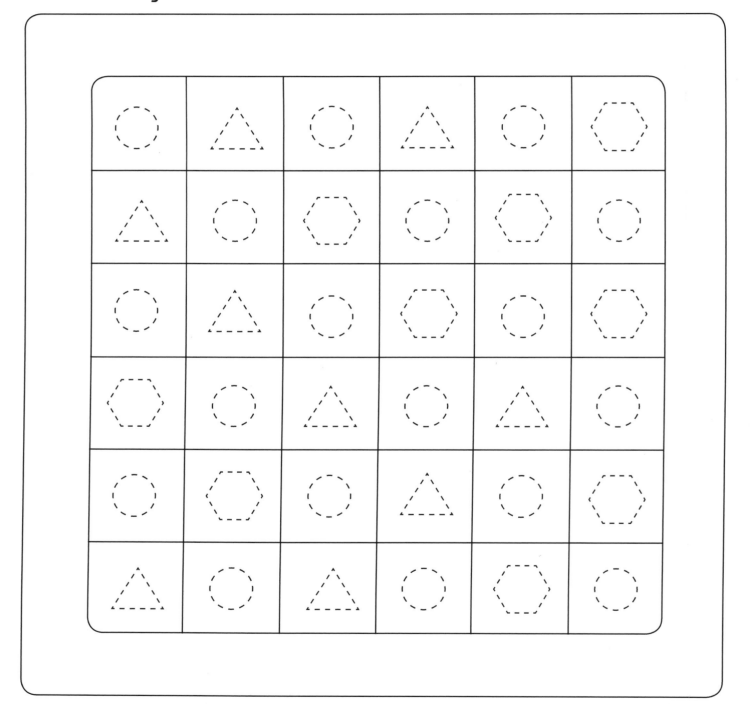

Name: _____   Date: _____

Color the boxes in the table following these rules:
- Squares are blue.   - Rectangles are yellow.
- Hexagons are orange.   - Triangles are red.
- Circles are green.

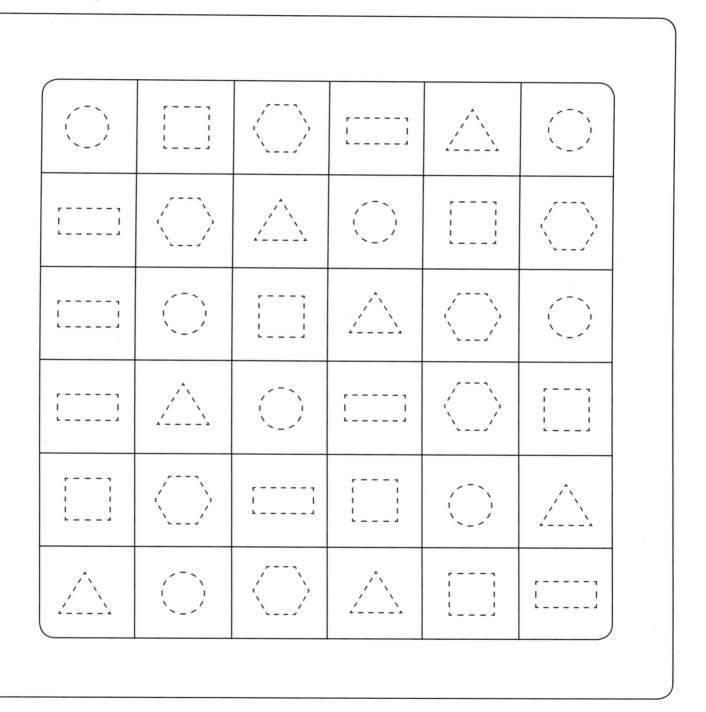

Name: _____   Date: _____

Going from left to right, circle all the squares that you find.

Going from left to right, circle all the triangles that you find.

Going from left to right, circle all the hexagons that you find.

Name: _____   Date: _____

Going from left to right, circle all the squares that you find.

Count the circles. How many are there? _____.

Color the circles blue.

Count the squares. How many are there? _____.

Color the squares red.

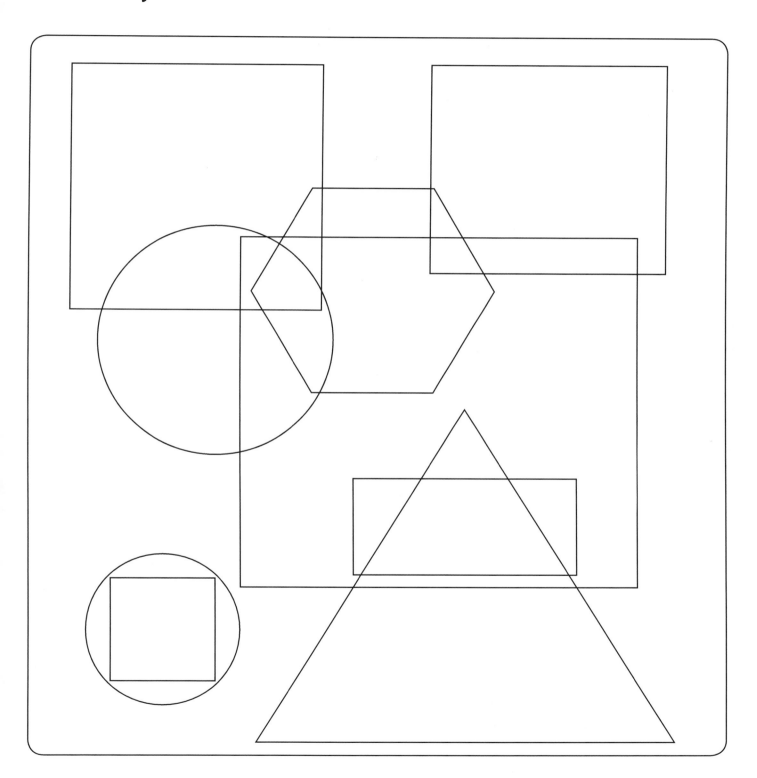

Name: _____   Date: _____

Count the rectangles. How many are there? _____.

Color the rectangles green.

Name: _____   Date: _____

Count the triangles. How many are there? _____.

Color the triangles yellow.

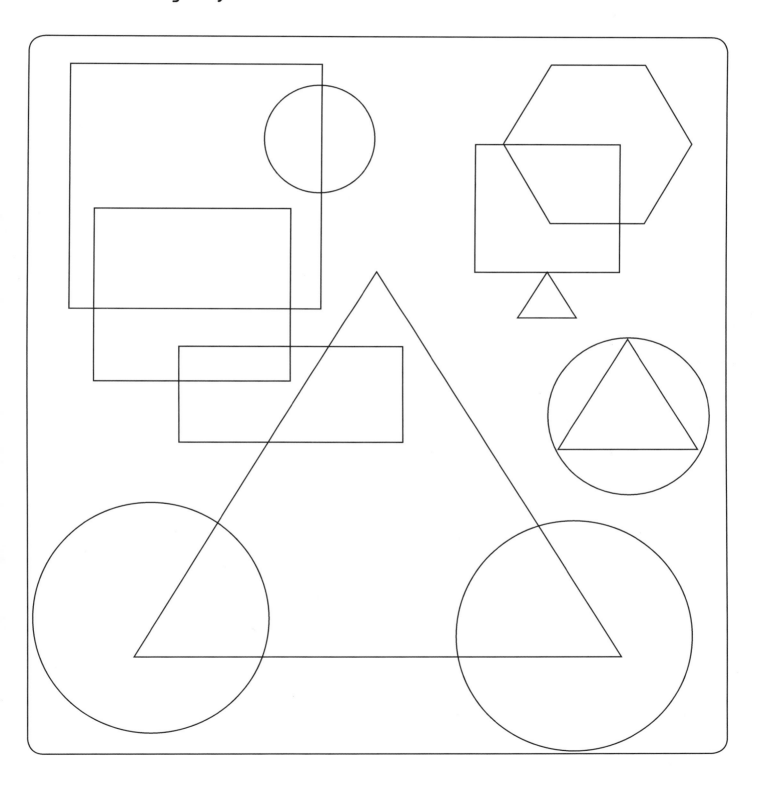

Count the hexagons. How many are there? _____.

Color the hexagons orange.

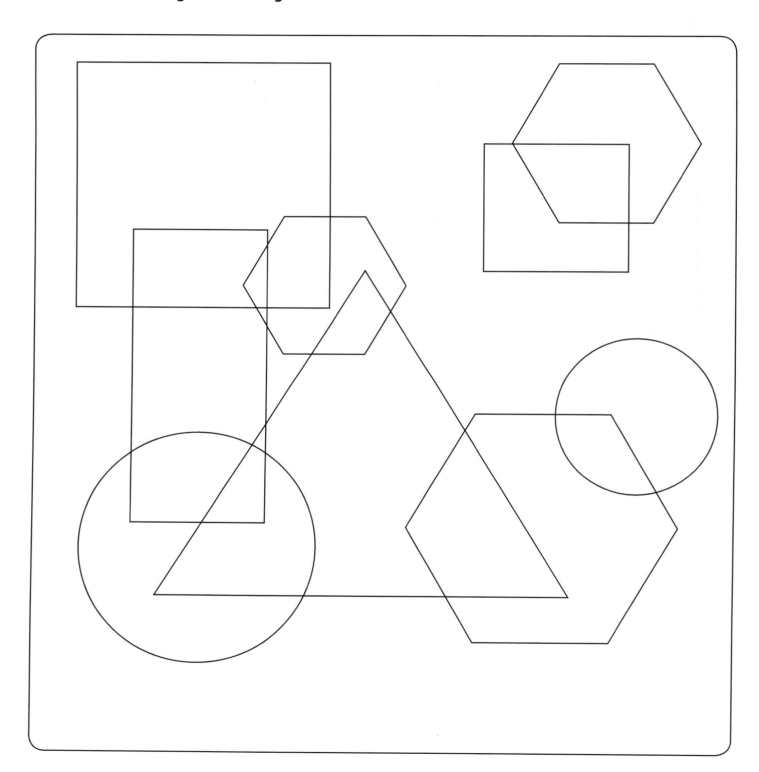

Name: _____ **Date:** _____

How many of each shape do you see?

 _____    _____    _____

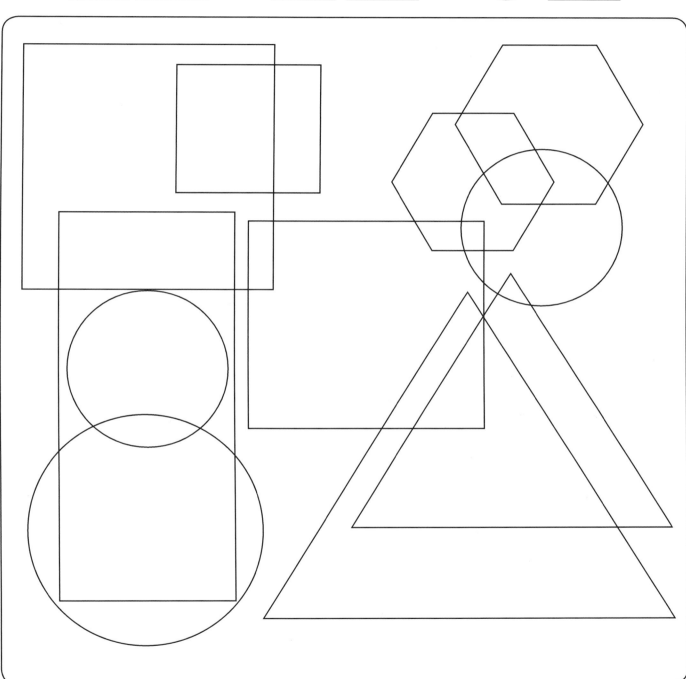

How many of each shape do you see?

How many of each shape do you see?

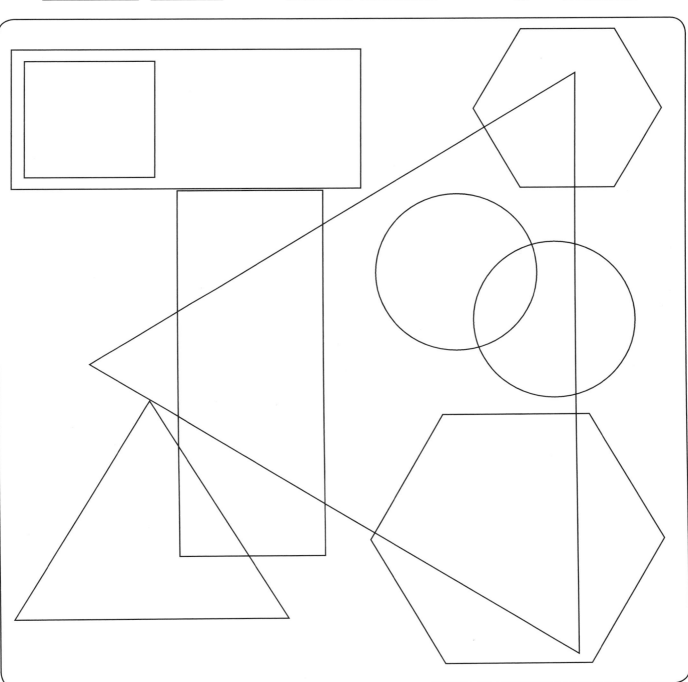

Name: _____   Date: _____

Color:

- the squares blue.   - the triangles red.

- the rectangles green.   - the circles yellow.

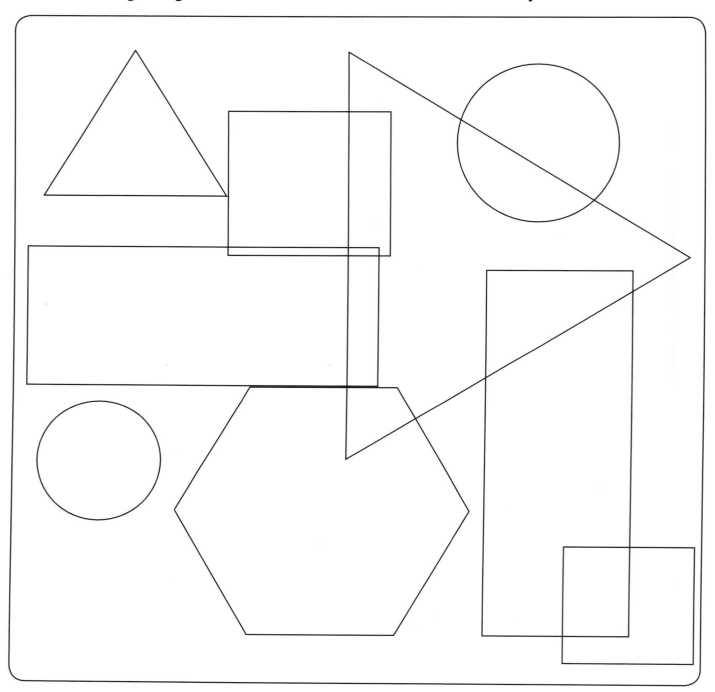

85388521R00057

Made in the USA
Middletown, DE
24 August 2018